Nell Riley
2729 S. Zinnia
Mesa, AZ 85209

D1711010

LITTLE
MADHOUSE
ON THE PRAIRIE

IT IS NOT THE TRUTH THAT WILL
HURT YOU — IT IS THE LIES.

Marion Witte

LITTLE
MADHOUSE
ON THE PRAIRIE

A True-Life Story of
Overcoming Abuse and
Healing the Spirit

MARION ELIZABETH WITTE

ANGEL HEART
Publishing
Ventura, California

Little Madhouse On The Prairie

Angel Heart Publishing, Inc.
P. O. Box 24557
Ventura, California 93002

Editorial services by Mark Bruce Rosin
Cover and book design by Barbara Obermeier Design
Printed in the United States of America

Copyright @ 2010 by Marion Elizabeth Witte

Publisher's Cataloging-in-Publication
(Provided by Quality Books, Inc.)

Witte, Marion Elizabeth.
Little madhouse on the prairie: a true-life story of
overcoming abuse and healing the spirit/Marion
Elizabeth Witte.
p. cm.
LCCN 2009913965
ISBN-13: 978-0-9822254-2-4
ISBN-10: 0-9822254-2-3
ISBN-13: 978-0-9822254-1-7
ISBN-10: 0-9822254-1-5

1. Witte, Marion Elizabeth. 2. Adult child abuse
victims–Biography. 3. Businesswomen–Biography.
4. Child abuse–Psychological aspects–Biography. 5.
Child abuse–Prevention–Biography. 6. Angel Heart
Foundation–Biography. 7. Adult child abuse victims'
writings,
American. I. Title.

HV6626.5.W58 2010 362.76
QBI10-600014

THIS BOOK IS DEDICATED TO

Oprah Winfrey

Who through her own courage and honesty
inspired me to tell my story

and

Child Advocates Around the World

Who work tirelessly to nurture and
protect our children

ACKNOWLEDGMENTS

To Beverly Yokum, for being my friend.

To Richard and Kress Darling,
who realized I could write this book long before I did.

To Mark Bruce Rosin,
who encouraged me to write and to cry,
sometimes at the same time.

To Angela Scaletta, for being my daughter.

CONTENTS

AUTHOR'S NOTE
13

VICTORIA
15

ONCE UPON A TIME
17

THE JOURNEY
115

LESSONS I LEARNED
183

AFTERWARD
221

BOOK CLUB DISCUSSION ITEMS
223

❧ Author's Note ❧

My intention in writing this book is help others heal. I have no desire to cause intentional harm to any person, or to cast anyone in the role of a villain.

I have changed the names of some of the non-family members mentioned in this book to protect their identity and dignity and to respect their privacy.

I have made every effort to report the details of my various life experiences with as much accuracy as possible, based on my age at the time of the event and my understanding of it today.

❧ VICTORIA ❧

Victoria is not her real name, as I want to protect her privacy. She is a sweet soul, with a sense of sadness about her. Her brown eyes reveal her mistrust.

I met her when I was volunteering at an after-school program in the Palm Springs, California area. Our aim for the three-month class was to instill the idea of self-empowerment in the children. The exercise we were working on that particular day involved writing an article describing something you liked about yourself. Victoria's head was bent over her paper and the pencil in her hand was not moving. I went over to her and asked her if I could see what she had written. She said - very vehemently I might add - "**NO!!**" I told her that was fine. This was a personal exercise, and she did not have to share her work.

Victoria was mistrustful, secretive and willful. I thought I was looking in the mirror!

I went around the room to work with the other children. Eventually we began to ask them to finish their project. I walked by Victoria, and I felt her strong little hand grab my wrist. Her left arm was lying on top of what she had written. She looked into my eyes, and then she moved her arm away from the paper. In her scribbled handwriting she had written:

"No little girl should have to live my life"

I choked back the tears and fought to keep my composure. I knelt down next to her. The little girl inside of me spoke to Victoria through my adult voice. "You are absolutely right. No little girl should have to struggle. I know it took a lot of courage for you to write what you did, and that courage will help you survive all of this." Tears welled up in her eyes, and in mine, and I hugged her as hard as I could.

At that moment, a voice whispered in my ear, "It's time to tell your story." And so I offer this book to Victoria, to you, and to all the children that it may help.

❧ ❧

❧ ONCE UPON A TIME ❧

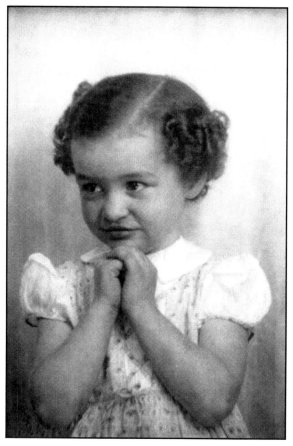

1951 Marion at three years
*My hair freshly permed. I pose angelically in the Wool-
worth's photo booth in 1951. How could this sweet
little three-year-old know she was on the verge of a
dark and painful future?*

ALL WE REALLY WANT
IS TO BE ACCEPTED AND LOVED.

Marion Witte

❧ THE FARM ❦

I was raised on the prairie of North Dakota in the 1950s in a dilapidated old farm house that had once served as the depot for the train station at Norpak, North Dakota. The railroad abandoned the station years before we moved to the farm, and the name of Norpak had been removed from any official area maps when the station closed. We were sharecroppers, which meant that we did not own the house where we lived or the land that we farmed. We grew and harvested the crops, and then we turned over half the proceeds from the sales to the landlord as our rental payment.

The first floor of our house contained a kitchen, a living room, a parlor and my mother and father's bedroom. The second floor had two bedrooms, one for my brother Frank, who was three years older than me, and the other for me and my sister Claudia, who was two years younger than me. The limited heat on the first floor came from the furnace that heated the living room, and there was no heating upstairs in the children's rooms. During the North Dakota brutal winters, the outdoor temperature often dropped to 30 degrees below. Any liquids in the upstairs bedrooms would freeze, so my sister and I would take our little perfume bottles downstairs during the winter months. When we woke in the morning, after a particularly cold night, the wallpaper in our bedroom would be covered with frost.

Indoor plumbing was installed when I was ten years old. Prior to that, we walked along a 25-foot path from the back porch off the kitchen to the outhouse, a small shed four feet wide and four feet long. The outhouse had no electricity and therefore no lighting, so at night it was pitch dark. During the winter everything froze, including what was deposited by the users, so being in the outhouse was tolerable. Summer was another story. The prairie heat caused everything to cook, and the odor in the outhouse was terrible. I would hold my breath as long as I could, and try to get in and out very quickly. There were times when I thought I might pass out from the stench, so instead of using the outhouse I would grab some toilet paper and go into the woods. I remember visiting nearby relatives who had a two-seater, and I was not impressed. I could not imagine having to spend time in an outhouse with another person. It was difficult enough being in there alone.

The North Dakota winter winds would blow ferociously, and the path to the outhouse would become hidden by snow. During these months of subzero weather, my father ran a rope between the house and the outhouse, and we would hold onto this lifeline in hopes of not getting lost or falling into the depths of a softened snow bank on our way to the outhouse.

Off the kitchen was an enclosed back porch and, although we had a front door, the family used the outside door to the porch as the main entrance to the house. Everyone left their shoes, outdoor coats, hats, and boots on the porch before opening the door that led into the kitchen. The porch also housed a chest-style freezer and an old washing machine with a wringer. Next to the washer was a big oak rod that my mother used to manually agitate the clothes in the washer. When not used for laundry purposes, this rod often served as the weapon of choice for punishments.

Next to the washing machine was a large, oval-shaped steel washtub. It was quite heavy and had metal handles on each end for lifting. Before my mother loaded my father's dirty work clothes into the washing machine, she would use an old-fashioned, corrugated steel washboard in the tub to scrub off the oil stains. The washtub was then used to carry a full load of wet laundry outside, where she hung it on the clothesline. During the winter months the smaller items were hung to dry on the rungs of a large wooden rack positioned over the furnace grate in the living room. In spite of the freezing temperatures, my mother continued to hang the bed linens on the outdoor clothesline, leaving them there until they became stiff. She would then bring the frozen sheets into the house, let them thaw out slightly, and use the mangle, her large ironing machine, to press them.

The washtub also functioned as the bathtub. Bathing was a once-a-week event for us, and we bathed in the kitchen. My mother would fill the washtub with a couple of gallons of water that had been warmed in pots on the kitchen stove. Another pan of water would be kept warm on the range top and used for rinsing purposes.

When my sister and I were small, we would take our baths together. Then my brother would bathe in the same water after we got out. As we got older, my sister would bathe first, then me, and finally my brother. By the time he stepped into the week's worth of muddy grey buildup my sister and I had deposited during our baths, the water had grown cold.

The older we got and the bigger we grew, the more difficult it became to fit in the tub. We would have to pull our knees up to our chests in order to sit down so that our mother could scrub us down with Lava soap. This grainy bar, with its powerful cleaning agent, was designed to remove farm machinery oil and grease from your hands. It served to remove any dirt I had accumulated and also the top layer of my skin, and I would exit the washtub covered with red blotches.

The kitchen was the focal point of our home, so family members would come and go during bath times. When I was little, this did not bother me, but as I grew older I became very conscious of this lack of privacy, and I would try to position the tub so that my back faced the door that led from the porch into the kitchen. I know the lack of privacy also bothered my brother. He and my mother got into a terrible fight when, at ten years old, he refused to bathe in the kitchen anymore. My mother tore off his clothes and dragged him by his arms to the tub, and shoved him into the tepid water. He lost that first battle, but I remember after that event he took his baths on the porch where my mother and father did their bathing in the tub. My baths remained in the kitchen until we got indoor plumbing.

The door from the porch into the kitchen would be closed most of the time to keep the cold air on the porch from seeping into the house. On the kitchen side of the door was a hanger with ten hooks, and it served as the closet for our school clothing when we had to dress in the kitchen because it was too cold to dress upstairs. By the time I was in third grade, my sister and I each had two or three dresses hanging there, and my brother had a couple of pairs of pants and shirts. Underwear and socks were stored in the chests of drawers in our rooms and, during the winter, were placed on the furnace grate to "take the freeze out of them" before we dressed.

The last hook at the end of the hanger on the kitchen door held a thick black leather belt. It was always there to be seen, whether you were eating a meal or taking a bath. Its presence served as a constant reminder of punishments that happened in the past and punishments yet to come.

The kitchen table looked as if it had been discarded from a 1940s roadside diner. The top was covered with gray-speckled Formica, and the edging and legs were molded chrome. The table was always covered with a plastic tablecloth with a floral pattern, and the salt and pepper shakers and butter dish were always kept on the table. The matching chairs had plastic-covered seats and backs. An old stove and oven, and an equally aged Frigidaire, rested against the back wall. In the middle of the kitchen counter was a rusty metal sink with a hand pump. Directly off of the kitchen was a food pantry, and on the floor of the pantry was a door leading to the cellar.

The kitchen floor was covered with linoleum, which my mother would wash and wax every week to an extremely high sheen. She would then cover it with newspapers and throw rugs to protect it from scratches. My father had impaired vision and on several occasions he would come into the kitchen and not see the freshly placed newspapers on the floor. When this happened, he would step onto the smooth paper in his stocking feet, which would slide out from under him. He would hit the floor with a loud thud, groan in pain, and swear to God as he got up. This usually preceded a fight with my mother, which led to my father leaving for the bar in town.

At one time, I believed that this is where it all started for me, on the prairies of North Dakota. As I came to discover later, that is not entirely true. It began at least two generations before, so I need to take you on a brief trip back to the past.

❧ WAY BACK WHEN ☙

In 1916, American women were getting closer to winning the right to vote and to being recognized as full citizens. Our country was months away from entering World War I (the Great War) in Europe to stop the aggression of Germany and its allies. And in Iowa, a young girl named Blanche Staver was about to engage in her own German battle. Events that unfolded in her life that year ultimately affected my destiny.

Blanche was born in Pennsylvania in 1900. When she was a young girl, her Dutch parents migrated with Blanche and their other children to Minnesota to seek employment as farm workers. As a teenager, Blanche was sent to work on the farm of relatives in Iowa. At the age of fifteen, while attending the local one-room schoolhouse, she was molested by her male teacher. This sexual abuse resulted in Blanche's becoming pregnant, and her relatives returned her to her parents in Minnesota. At sixteen, Blanche gave birth to a baby girl, and she named her Ruby Mae.

In the area where the Stavers lived, the Red River ran along the border between Minnesota and North Dakota. The bachelor farmer Frank Witte lived on the North Dakota side of the river, immediately west of the Staver's farmhouse. Frank's birth name was Franz, and he was born in Germany, the second oldest of twelve children. In 1896, at the age of seventeen, Franz and an uncle boarded the German ship *Havel* bound for the United States. Franz paid for his passage by caring for the mules being transported for sale. When he arrived in New York, he changed his name to Frank and set off on a journey to the Midwest with his uncle, a priest being assigned to a German parish in Illinois. Frank lived and worked in Illinois and Iowa before settling in North Dakota, where at first he worked as a farmhand for a German family with twelve children of their own. He learned the agricultural business and, after several years, acquired his own farmstead and established a horse-trading business. Frank worked hard and he played harder. Those who knew him described him as charming, gregarious, authoritarian, and a drinker. And not necessarily in that order.

As destiny played out, Blanche Staver's life was about to change radically one more time. As a sixteen-year-old girl with a three-month-old baby in her care, Blanche did not fit into the black-and-white moralistic view that existed at that time. Her parents decided that the proper course of action was for Blanche to marry Frank Witte, who by that time had turned into a 37-year-old taskmaster with a temper and a drinking problem. Once the matter of Blanche's marriage was settled upon, her parents moved back to Pennsylvania. And Blanche settled down to a life that was undoubtedly different from the one that she had dreamed of as a young girl. After being molested by an older male authority figure, she now found herself married off to the same type of person.

Frank and Blanche Witte would eventually become my grandparents, and the ancestral tinderbox of abuse, alcoholism, violence, and abandonment was ignited.

Blanche bore Frank five of his own children, thereby creating a workforce for their farming operations. By the time my grandmother was 27 years old, she had six young children to care for, along with the demanding duties of a farm housewife. Frank treated Blanche like she was one of the children, in large part because of the 21-year age difference. His abuse and alcoholism added to the direness of her circumstances. Blanche Staver Witte was indeed living in a personal war zone.

Frank refused to adopt or even accept Blanche's three-month-old baby, therefore Ruby's last name was Staver instead of Witte. He referred to Ruby Mae as his "bastard daughter," and he had an abusive, tumultuous relationship with her during the time she remained in his house. Viewing Blanche as a child, Frank did not feel that she deserved to be listened to, and she was unable to protect Ruby from him. At the age of fourteen, Ruby dropped out of school, and by sixteen she was no longer able to tolerate her living conditions. Blanche proposed that Ruby go live with her grandparents, and so Ruby moved out of Frank's house and headed for the Staver's home in Pennsylvania.

My father, Alvin, was Blanche and Frank's second oldest child, and he was very fond of his sister Ruby. While Ruby lived with them, my father had tried to protect her as best he could, even at the expense of Frank abusing him. No matter what his father Frank thought of Ruby, to my father she was a sister that he cared for deeply. Their bond lasted their entire lives, until they died over 70 years later, within a month of each other.

Looking back with the knowledge I have gained as an adult about my family history, the patterns I see are striking. When Blanche was sixteen years old and pregnant as a result of rape, her parents brokered her off to an available husband. When Blanche's daughter was sixteen and Frank still refused to accept her, Ruby Mae was shipped off to live with her grandparents. Problems in our family got "solved" through abandonment. It is also striking that both my grandmother Blanche and my aunt Ruby Mae were forced into adulthood when they were sixteen years old. That age would also turn out to be an important one in my life.

When Ruby Mae was 25, she returned to North Dakota with her five-year-old son, Jim, to visit her mother. By that time, Ruby had married my uncle Lou, an outgoing young man from the same small Pennsylvania town where she had lived with her grandparents. Lou did not accompany Ruby on her trip back to North Dakota because he had to stay home to work. Frank Witte was assigned the task of "fetching" Ruby and Jim at the bus station in Fargo, a duty that he probably resented because of his animosity toward Ruby and her child. Prior to Ruby and Jim's scheduled arrival at 8:00 in the morning, Frank spent the entire night at the local bar, drinking and playing poker with his friends. He left the bar at 6:30 a.m. and drove toward Fargo. En route, he lost control of his car and it plunged into a steep ravine. A passerby discovered him in that gulch and called for an ambulance to take him to the hospital in Fargo, where he died shortly after admission. My grandfather was 62 years old when he killed himself driving drunk in the early hours of the morning. Ruby Mae and Jim were retrieved later that morning at the bus station by Blanche, who related the events of the morning to her daughter. Ruby attempted to console her mother, who was in a state of distress. Years later Ruby Mae revealed that she too had been upset, not because of Frank's untimely death, but because the visit to see her mother was marred by having to attend the funeral of the man she used to call her arch-enemy.

In my mind, Frank Witte's final act was a gift to Ruby Mae, whom he had forced out of his house so many years before. By dying before he reached the station, he eliminated the possibility that she and her son would be passengers in his car while he was driving drunk back to his farm. Ruby Mae and Jim avoided dying at his hands on that country road, so it appears that Ruby's guardian angel was looking out for her that day.

Frank died in 1941, the year the United States entered World War II in Europe. Ironically, Blanche did not have to wait four years for her victory over the Germans. The personal war in which she was engaged came to an abrupt end with Frank's death.

My Aunt Ruby was the most willing of the siblings to share her childhood experiences with me, and it is from her that I came to understand that my grandfather was abusive not only to her, but to his two oldest sons, my Uncle Bernard and my father, Alvin. My father's two younger sisters were very cautious about what they would divulge to me, but they acknowledged that their father would take out his anger primarily on Bernard and my father, and, until she left, on Ruby. They saw Frank beat their brothers many times. They also admitted that they witnessed their mother being belittled and humiliated by Frank, and treated like a child in front of all of them. My father would offer very little information when I questioned him about his father and his childhood. He would squirm in his chair and mumble that he didn't remember too much about Frank, except that "he was tough." My father was trained to "keep quiet" and "not tell" long before I was schooled in the tradition of silence.

My mother's parents, Oliver and Josephine Serum, were Norwegians, a nationality not known for extensive communication skills. Their language was clipped, and my mother's family used as few words as possible, perhaps reflecting the harsh environment in which they lived. My personal assessment is that they believed too much time spent talking would take away from the time you could be working. My mother's ancestors were not big talkers, but they were wonderful workers.

Oliver Serum was born in Minnesota in 1880, the second oldest of nine children in a family that farmed on the east side of the Red River. Oliver wed Josephine Rognlie when he was 30 and she was 21. A few years into their marriage, they moved to Washington State, where Oliver worked in a relative's grocery store for three years. Then he decided to move his family to Minneapolis, Minnesota, to start his own mom-and-pop grocery store. Two years later, Oliver's father became ill and could no longer farm. My grandfather's three brothers had not survived the Great War, so Oliver felt an obligation to move back to the farm and run it for his family. My grandfather, known as Papa to his children, lived and farmed in the frigid cold of the Minnesota prairie until he contracted pneumonia during the winter of 1929. Papa was taken by horse and sleigh to the rail station for transport to Fargo. He died at the age of 49, immediately upon arriving at the hospital, just as the Great Depression started.

Josephine was born in the Dakota Territory in 1889, shortly before it became a state. She was the youngest of eleven children, three dying in infancy. After marrying Oliver, she gave birth to the four children she would have by the age of 29. My mother was her fifth and last child, born when Grandma was 37. Tragically, my grandfather died less than three years later, leaving my grandmother with five children to raise and a large farm to manage.

I wonder what it must have been like for my grandmother Josephine, a young woman, to leave the city of Minneapolis, with its modern conveniences and opportunities for a social life and entertainment, and move to an obscure, primitive prairie homestead. Life in Minneapolis included electricity, running water, and indoor bathrooms. The farmhouse, by contrast, was lit by gas lanterns, water was pumped by hand, and the only bathrooms were outhouses. My grandfather felt it was his responsibility to his family to return to the farm, and my grandmother was expected to participate in fulfilling what he saw as his duty.

I also wonder about the impact on her of his early death. She was a pioneering woman, and had become accustomed to hard work and adversity, yet I cannot help thinking that she might have harbored resentment about her circumstances. She had been isolated on a prairie farm and then, after her husband's death, she had been left to fend for herself and her children. If my grandmother had regrets about not living a different life, she suffered in silence. As history played out, my mother would wind up following in her mother's footsteps. She also found herself on an isolated prairie farm, abandoned by her husband.

❧ THE FAMILY TREE IN OUR YARD ❧

My mother's father died when she was two-and-a-half years old, and my mother has no memory of him, nor did she hear much about him from her mother. My mother believes that by the time she was old enough to be included in conversations, everybody was tired of talking about him. As a child, she worked on the farm along with her brothers and sisters, helping with the egg collection duties. That task would later be assigned to me during my childhood.

My mother's mother and father both came from intellectual lineages. Three of my mother's aunts graduated from college in the early 1900s, a rare achievement for women in those days. My mother received her fair share of genius and she graduated from high school at the age of sixteen, although she did not go to college because her mother could not afford to send her. Even without a formal education beyond high school, she accumulated a vast amount of information through reading, and she had a large vocabulary and would finish crossword puzzles in a matter of minutes.

My father was the third of six children raised on the Witte farm in North Dakota. Dad was allowed to go to school through the sixth grade, and then he had to quit in order to work full time on the family farm. He and his siblings had a difficult life, being used as child labor on the farm and growing up in a household with their angry, alcoholic father.

When my father was three years old, he and his five-year-old brother, Bernard, and six-year-old sister, Ruby Mae, were clearing rocks from one of the fields to prepare it for planting. My grandfather used dynamite sticks to blow up the larger boulders so that the children could then transport the smaller pieces. The children found some explosives that had not detonated and at the end of the day they took them back to the house. Curious to see what would happen, they threw the dynamite into the fire of the wood stove in the kitchen. The explosion that followed blinded my father, blew off the tips of the fingers on one hand of his brother, and caused Ruby Mae to become deaf in one ear. For almost five years, my father was totally blind and had to be led around by his siblings, a gauze bandage wrapped around his head. During this time, my father and his brother, Bernard, developed an inseparable bond that lasted their whole lives. At age eight, my father's bandages were removed and he received a glass eye. Partial vision had returned in the remaining eye.

My mother and father grew up in adjacent farming communities; she on the Minnesota side of the Red River, he on the North Dakota side. They married when she was 17 and he was 24 in a rural Roman Catholic Church. My father was raised under the strict rules and regulations of Catholicism, just as his father had been in Germany. My mother attended the Lutheran Church as a child but converted to Catholicism prior to marrying my father. Catholics were not allowed to marry outside of their religion in those days, so an interfaith marriage would have been unacceptable to my father and his family. This potential problem was avoided, as my mother changed faiths in order to marry my father. The tie that bound them together for almost 58 years was their unwavering devotion to their religion.

Immediately after the wedding, my mother and father traveled to California to spend the winter visiting my father's mother,

Blanche, who had moved there with some of his younger siblings the year before. My mother loved the exciting life, the interesting people, and especially the weather in California, so she wanted to remain there to live. My father was anxious to get back to North Dakota to resume his farming duties with his brother, Bernard. In much the same way as her mother had when she had been forced to leave Minneapolis for her husband's family's prairie farm, my mother got a taste of life away from the prairie only to have to submit to her husband's desire to return to an isolated farmhouse.

As I mentioned, my father said almost nothing about his father. Indeed, he spoke very little about his childhood. I sensed that he loved his mother, yet I wonder if he lost respect for Blanche, and maybe all women, as he watched Frank belittle her and as he watched Blanche choose to send his beloved sister Ruby Mae away rather than stand up to her husband. Based on the history I have been able to gather, in some ways my father was much like his father. They were both gregarious, charming alcoholics and gamblers, and they liked to tease and flirt with women other than their wives. And they were both angry men. My grandfather had a temper that caused him to explode at others; my father preferred to implode on himself. Angry parents breed angry children, and I would come to understand this in the most intimate way.

As I look back, I think my mother suffered from depression. I did not understand this as a child, as all Norwegians seemed sullen and withdrawn to me since they were short on conversation and displayed little emotion. The most common expression they used was Uf dah — literally meaning "Oh my"—and it was said with very little feeling. It served as a universal response to every comment from "It's sure hot today" to "Did you see the Johnson's new tractor?" to "The barn is burning down."

My mother was different from the other Scandinavians in that, between bouts of work, she slept a lot. She slept when we played outside, she slept all afternoon on the weekends, and, looking back, I think she probably slept when we were at school. I remember once when I was a teenager asking my father why she slept so much. He said she was just tired. Later on as an adult, I came to agree with him, except I believe she was tired of her life. By the time she was 24, she had three children under the age of five and she prepared all the meals for her family and for the four or five men working in the fields during the harvesting season. Cooking for that many people is a staggering amount of work for one woman—and she did laundry, cleaned, and watched her husband head off for the bar at night, where he would drink and play pinochle.

If I had had her life, I would have been depressed too.

❧ Mommy and Me ❦

My mother was the disciplinarian in the family, a job she took on with a vengeance. My father's constant absence from the house allowed her free rein over the household and the children. She assumed the entire responsibility of administering punishment in our house, which turned out to be the perfect outlet for her suppressed rage and anger. The consistent factor in our punishment was its inconsistency. Every day, every hour, and every minute we could be punished for doing something that previously had not provoked a punishment. It seemed to come out of nowhere, like a force out of the darkness.

As a small child, I tried to determine what I did that "made Mommy mad," and then I tried desperately not to do that again. I discovered that there was always something new or different that I did to bring about her wrath, so I was not able to correlate my behavior with her response. The outbursts were often random, and without an explanation that made sense as to what I had done to provoke such rage. I spent a lot of time observing my Mommy's expressions and trying to gauge her moods to see if it was safe to stay visible, or whether it was time to hide. I was often fooled, as a laugh from her one minute could turn into a spewing of anger and viciousness the next. Sometimes she would seem relaxed and at ease going about her chores, and then, the very next instant, she would go out of control, she would scream at me and beat me until her rage subsided. I was totally at her mercy.

Many times her outbursts happened in the kitchen. When we felt we might be safe, and the mood in the kitchen was pleasant, my brother and I would "goof around" while we were finishing our meal at the table. Often my father would have already gone off to the bar in town after finishing his meal, or he may not have eaten dinner with us, choosing instead to eat at the restaurant in Mapleton, as he did on several occasions. As our mother cleared off the table, my brother loved to make me laugh by belching as loud as he could. Or sometimes he performed his favorite trick, turning his eyelids inside out so that I would scream out in disgust. Many times these antics ended pleasantly, with my brother and I being allowed to laugh a little before we asked my mother for the obligatory permission to leave the table. Other times we did not fare so well. If my mother decided that either my brother's behavior or my response offended her, the harshest of punishment could be meted out. Though she seldom gave us an explanation of what we had done wrong, we were both too terrified of her to ask why.

When my brother was selected as the target, my mother would instruct me to remain sitting at the table and watch in silence as she beat him with whatever instrument was handy. Sometimes that was a large wooden spoon, sometimes the cast iron skillet, sometimes the belt on the hanger on the back of the inside door from the front porch. And sometimes it was her hands. She would often make him pull his pants down, and he would dutifully bend over the chair and remain relatively quiet while she struck him over and over, as many as fifteen or twenty times. Her face would be red and contorted with anger as she inflicted her blows. My brother would yelp once in a while, yet he never gave her the satisfaction of breaking into tears or sobbing. When she was finished, he would stand up, pull up his pants, his eyes lowered in deep embarrassment. I barely looked at him, and often I would be holding back the tears welling up in my eyes.

While he was being beaten, I tried to block out the sounds in the room, so I would focus on any sound coming from outside, like the dog barking or, if the beating was during the day, the roar of the engines of farm machinery. If I showed any signs of crying, my mother would scream at me, "If you want to be a crybaby, come over here and I will give you something to cry about!" I would hold in the tears and sit quietly until she gave me permission to leave the table.

Watching my brother being abused seemed more horrifying to me than the dreadfulness of my own punishments. During my punishments, I felt that I could control, at least to some extent, my feelings and emotions. But I felt absolutely powerless, unable to help him in any way, as I sat quietly witnessing his pain and anguish. Being a party to such a horrific event, even unwillingly, engendered deep feelings of guilt in me that I carried for many years.

If I was the chosen offender, I bore similar punishments, and occasionally my brother was forced to sit and watch. When I was a small child, I would cry out in pain from the blows of her hand, the spatula, or whatever object she used. I cried out because it hurt—physically and emotionally. As I grew older, I became desensitized to the physical pain, and frequently I would remain silent during the beatings. I would let my mind wander, often to plans of what I was going to do to my mother when I grew up. My lack of response frequently infuriated her, and she would attack me even harder. Although I knew that crying out in anguish gave her the satisfaction of knowing that I was in pain, and by doing so the punishment would end sooner, I did not care. I learned to follow my brother's lead. I believe our silence was an unconscious display of a small act of defiance during these much larger acts of violence.

Sometimes instead of lashing out on the spur of the moment, my mother announced prior to the punishment that she was going to punish us. When this happened just enough time elapsed between her declaration and the act so that we suffered severe anxiety while waiting for the beating. Announced punishments often included the requirement that I fetch the weapon of choice, whether it was the leather belt hanging next to my little green dress on the back of the door or the oak rod standing by the washing machine. My mother's demeanor was much colder during these punishments, as she had time to methodically think about her attack.

My mother's displays of rage, couched in the guise of punishment, were a common occurrence in our house. It took me a while to realize that they never happened when my father was home. When Dad was around, she might raise her voice if she got angry at us, yet she would never physically punish us in his presence.

I became terrified of my mother, both because of the abuse and because I never knew when she would lose control and blow up. I felt as though I was a character in one of those games you find at a pizza parlor or a carnival. A plastic chipmunk or squirrel randomly pops up and down while the contestant waits with a rubber mallet in hand for the chance to whack the poor rodent before it can go underground again. I was the target and my mother the contestant during my childhood, and I lost that game many times as my mother whacked me down.

I mentioned that the floor of the kitchen was always polished to a high sheen. I was amazed by the care my mother took to make sure that every spill was immediately cleaned up, along with any dust or dirt that came in from the back porch. Mom baked bread and pies, and many times I would be required to sit and quietly watch as she kneaded the dough and then rolled it out to use as a pie crust or shaped it into the bread pan. This experience was not unpleasant, since often the kitchen would be filled with delicious aromas drifting from the oven.

Other times, as I lay bent over one of the kitchen chairs awaiting a beating, my eyes would follow the pattern embossed in the linoleum or focus on the texture or color of the throw rugs that protected the floor's glossy shine. The sweet smell of pie often permeated the room, and I would take in deep breaths to fully inhale the rich aroma. I would listen carefully to make out the sounds of the farm machinery in the fields. And I would wonder.

I would wonder why the floor that my mother had worked so hard to shine was better cared for than I was. I wondered why the pie-making process got more attention than I did. And I wondered why no one ever beat the farm machinery. And then one day I stopped wondering, for I came to believe that the floor, the pie, and the tractors were much more important than me.

Many years later, I started to comprehend the devastating emotional effects this abuse had on me. And not until recently did I begin to really understand my mother, and to realize that the rage she took out on me had nothing at all to do with me.

✥ BECOMING A "WILLFUL" CHILD ✥

By the time I was five years old, I had given up the fruitless task of trying to figure out what I could do to stay on my mother's good side. I began planning my actions and behavior based on what seemed right for me as opposed to what might align with her capricious rules. This resulted in my mother calling me a "willful" child. I depended heavily on my new internal guidance, although no voice in my head delivered this information and it had no physical manifestation that I could discern. It definitely was not something I was taught. The best way I can describe it is to give it the name "knowingness."

The more I connected to this knowingness, the more I made decisions for myself, and the more my mother called me willful. The more she called me willful, the more I exercised my will, and the more dangerous the world became for me because of how she reacted. In spite of everything my mother did, by five years old I was not about to allow anyone "to make me do what they wanted." I would accept my punishment of going hungry all day rather than take up my mother's offer to blame my brother for something I had done. I would incur a beating with the one-inch-diameter oak stick rather than admit to something I did not do. And I would watch the welts rise from a strapping with a black leather belt rather than agree to listen to my mother and wear my brother's hand-me-down overalls. Dressing was a common battleground between us. My mother often demanded I dress as she instructed, and if I did not, during the ensuing spanking she would scream at me, "We're too poor to afford girl's clothing and you're lucky to have clothes at all!"

After the fight ended, I would mentally determine which one of us had "won the battle." If I decided it was me, I would stand on one of the kitchen chairs on my tiptoes, reach up to the hanger on the kitchen door, and pick out my favorite dress from the three hanging there. It was a gift from my Grandmother, who had made it for me during a summer stay with her. She had allowed me to pick out the fabric at the five-and-dime store and I had chosen a green flowered print for the bodice and a solid-green cotton for the skirt. It had puffy little sleeves and an attached belt that tied in the back. I wore that little dress many, many days during my childhood. I also wore it long after it was too short and too tight for my growing body.

As I grew, my will continued to grow stronger right along with me, and it provided the strength I needed to never give up and to keep myself alive. The scars I incurred for my willfulness are a roadmap of my life as child. The scars also hold memories. Sometimes, when I touch a scar, the events that caused it come flooding back to me. Other times, when I gently massage a scarred area, it is actually a pleasant feeling. I can only surmise that scar tissue holds both the feeling of the trauma and the feeling of the healing. Many of the scars from my childhood left no physical mark; they came from mental and emotional abuse just as real and tangible as a beating.

❧ THE CELLAR ❧

As I grew older, sometimes my mother would engage my brother in carrying out my punishment. An offense worthy of a serious reprimand, such as "sassing back," would have harsh repercussions, one of them being locked in the cellar. I would obey my mother's command to walk into the pantry and wait while my brother opened the cellar door so that I could descend the stairs. I do not remember being upset with my brother for his involvement. I told myself that he was only following orders and he would not harm me on his own. Soon enough I would find out that I was wrong about that.

The pantry was adjacent to the kitchen. Flour, sugar and canned goods lined the wooden shelves, along with purchases from the Watkins Company. The traveling salesman, whom we children fondly called the "Watkins Man," would stop at the farm monthly, selling the seasonings, spices, baking goods and fruit punch mix he carried in his truck.

The cellar door was in the floor of the pantry. It was about three feet by six feet, and one side of it was hinged to the floor. My mother or brother opened it by pulling up on a large metal ring on the door, and then waited while I carefully descended the ladder-like stairs that led from the pantry into the darkness of the cellar.

The cellar was basically a dirt dug-out that provided a cold storage area for canned goods and potatoes. There were no windows. A single light bulb hung from the ceiling and its pull chain dangled from the fixture. It was impossible for a small child like me to reach the chain, so when I was in the cellar, it was absolutely dark. No light seeped in around the edges of the overhead door. It was stark, abject darkness. My brother, or sometimes my younger sister, was given the job of standing on the cellar door so I could not open it from underneath. It would have made no difference if it had not been sealed in this manner; my terror was enough to make me a prisoner. I was five years old when my mother first made me go down to the cellar. Even as I write this, the hairs on the back of my neck rise in a replay of that terror.

In the darkness and silence, I heard the scratching and scurrying of the mice and rats that infested the cellar. At times, I thought I saw their eyes staring at me. Sitting on one of the rungs of the ladder, I would pull my legs up to my chest as tightly as I could. I thought if I didn't breathe maybe those little demons would not hear me, and they would not bite at my toes. I became an expert at not breathing.

The first time I remember experiencing what I have come to think of as "leaving my body" was in the cellar. I can best describe this as a disassociation of thoughts and emotions from the experience. I was fully awake and aware of what was happening, yet it was as though I was an observer of the event instead of the one experiencing it. My physical senses seemed to be dulled, and although I could still see and hear, I had little feeling or emotion about what was occurring. This technique, which I believe my mind developed as a survival tool, was out of my control. It would automatically take over at times when I experienced extreme pain, terror, or danger. When I "returned" from one of these episodes, I would often still be experiencing the physical pain but have no conscious recollection of any feelings that were associated with the event. As I later came to understand, the emotional aspect of the memory had been deeply buried in my unconscious, where it affected my behavior and my deepest feelings about myself in the most insidious and harmful ways.

When I was in the cellar and did not "leave my body," I sat on the stairs and had many thoughts about myself. "I was bad." "I was unworthy." "I was unlovable." I never saw my brother or sister being put in the cellar, so I thought there must be something terribly wrong with me. I thought these thoughts, sitting in the dark on the wooden stairs, and I held on to these ideas, even though they were untrue, throughout many of my adult years. The cellar abuse stopped when I was eight, but I continued to abuse myself with my cellar thinking for years to come. The cellar was a perfect representation of the isolation and abandonment I felt as a small child. And having continually experienced this as a youngster, it became very natural for me to find situations and environments that recreated these experiences well into my adult life.

❧ THE CARD GAME ❧

My mother's oldest sister, Iola, lived on a farm in Minnesota about an hour from our house. I did not enjoy visits to her house because my aunt always displayed a cool attitude toward me. I think she sensed that I did not trust her, and, in truth, I did not. I could not understand why she stood by while my uncle was so cruel to one of her sons.

My uncle Lafe was one of the family's alcoholic members, a rather large subset of the tribe. He frightened me when he was sober, and when he got drunk, he scared me to death.

Our family gatherings usually revolved around a meal. My aunt was a very good cook, and there was always a lot to eat. She would cook the dinner, and my mother would bring the dessert, usually one of her apple or sour cream raisin pies. When the meal ended, my aunt and my mother would clear the table and wash and dry the dishes in the kitchen. My uncle and my father would go into the living room and drink their coffee and smoke cigarettes.

In those days, women wore dresses all of the time. I remember my mother having a dress on at home when she was vacuuming or scrubbing the floor. For dinners at my aunt's house, both my aunt and my mother would be wearing their Sunday-best dresses, completing the look with high heels and nylon stockings. During these visits, my mother laughed and joked with her sister and they both acted like they had a perfect life and perfect families.

After the women had finished their work in the kitchen, someone would set up the portable card table for that evening's game, usually bridge, canasta, or whist. These were games of strategy, and winning seemed very important. Criticism would be dished out if one of the players made a play that was not clever enough.

One night, I was sitting quietly in a chair by the card table while my brother and the younger cousin played games in another room. My dad and uncle were consuming alcohol while they played cards. As I sat watching the grownups, I looked around the table and my eyes rested on my uncle. He had just finished his drink, and he was getting up to go into the kitchen for a refill. As he walked away, my eyes drifted to a figure under the table. It was my older cousin, Orlind.

Orlind was thin and lanky, and he had a wonderful laugh and twinkling eyes. In spite of Orlind's charm, it seemed that in his father's eyes he could do nothing right. My uncle routinely subjected him to harsh punishments, and my aunt did not intervene to stop them. She was, in my eyes, a co-tormentor.

My uncle had ordered my cousin to lie on the floor near his feet, which afforded Lafe the opportunity to occasionally strike Orlind in the head with his boot. When my uncle returned to the table after refilling his drink, he sat down and kicked Orlind in the ribs. I heard him say "If you're going to act like a dog, I'm going to treat you like a dog."

I looked around the room, stopping at the mounted head of a deer that my uncle had killed on one of his hunts. The deer had a full head of antlers and large, brown, glazed-over eyes. He had been placed on display as the prize of the latest kill. Even back then, I realized I had a lot in common with that creature hanging on the wall. We had the same dark brown eyes, staring intently, waiting for the kill.

My little eyes then moved back to the table, and I focused on the four adults, one at a time. They were talking about farming and gossiping about other people in the family. The men were drinking and everyone was laughing and having a great time. And all the while, my poor cousin was crouched under the table like a wounded animal, with no one coming to rescue him. Already defeated, Orlind knew his place. Under the table.

I was a very young girl as I sat there in my chair watching this, yet the picture of my cousin under the table has remained in my head and heart for decades. I questioned my father about this event much later in our lives, when he and I were able to have open discussions. He filled in many details about that particular card game. My father said that "back then" everyone minded their own business, and you did not get involved in how anybody else raised their children. His voice was quivering as he spoke, and I sensed the guilt and shame in his words, for my cousin Orlind had grown up to be an alcoholic and he spent time in and out of mental institutions and prisons, and for much of his life he was homeless.

Sadly, my father also chose not to intervene in my life either.

❧ DADDY AND ME ❧

As I mentioned, the furnace underneath the living room provided the only heat for the entire house. Occasionally, when everybody else was in bed, my father and I would each take a child-sized chair and sit on the grate that covered the furnace. The two identical chairs belonged to my sister and me. They were Early American in style and well constructed of solid wood stained a dark walnut color. The seats had no cushions and the backs were made from five wooden dowels. The chairs always wobbled a little on the uneven surface of the furnace grate. Because he was too big to be comfortable in the chair if he sat in it normally, my father would sit backwards, his arms wrapped around the chair back. He smoked constantly, lighting his next cigarette from the soon-to-be extinguished embers of the current one. He smelled of cigarette smoke all of the time, and of beer most of the time.

With people outside the family, my father was gregarious. He was a great conversationalist with a wonderful sense of humor. After church on Sundays, he always stopped to talk to friends and neighbors. He loved teasing people. I would listen as he chastised one of his fellow farmers for placing only five dollars in the collection basket. He would tell him that was not a very big donation, considering the farmer had a great crop this year. The listener would become solemn and eye my father, trying to see if he was serious. My father would wait ten seconds or so, then break out in a belly laugh and grab his friend's shoulder in a show of affection, confirming that he was just teasing.

My father also had a way of engaging people in a unique, subtle interview process, which resulted in their opening up to him. In many ways, he was a natural therapist. He was also generous, giving freely of any extra money when he had it, and always giving his time. He had great compassion for people with problems. He was especially social when he was with his friends and his drinking buddies, so they became the beneficiaries of these wonderful aspects of his personality. Unfortunately, he did not share these incredible qualities with me as a child, and I do not think he understood how desperately I wanted him to. As I reflect on this today, I believe my father knew little about what would make a child happy, as he never experienced happiness himself as a little boy.

And so, during our time on the furnace grate, we mostly

sat in silence. As I looked around the dimly lit living room, I noticed the curlicue figures in the worn carpeting and the wallpaper with its colored flowers. These quiet stretches were broken when the furnace motor started up with a click, followed by a whir and then the blast of warm air coming up through the grate. When I was barefoot, I would try to keep my feet on the thin rung of my chair so that heat would not burn my feet. If I was wearing socks or slippers, I would put my feet directly on the grate, until I could bear the heat no longer. I would then have to move my chair onto the carpet, and then bend over the heat and rub my hands together to keep warm. My father never moved off of the furnace. Either the heat did not bother him, or he was caught up in his own thoughts. This was the warmest I ever felt during the wintertime in that house.

During the summer months, when the weather was at its best, after supper my father would often sit on the front step of our house, smoking his cigarette and gazing off into the fields before he set out for the bar in town. Sometimes I would join him on the step, sitting quietly, watching him watch the sunset. I would wait until he turned to look at me, as this was my cue that it was okay to talk to with him. One time I ventured out on a limb and I asked him if we were poor. He looked over at me and replied, "Yes, we are. You need to know that there is no shame in being poor, but it is damned embarrassing."

I know that my father loved me, certainly not the way I wanted him to, but still he loved me. He would call me his "princess" and I have memories of him carrying me around in his big arms when I was very young. That adoration cost me dearly. I believe my mother was very jealous of the love and attention my father gave me, as their own relationship was anything but warm and loving. Sometimes my spankings would be accompanied with her sarcastically delivered comment, "What does Daddy's little princess think of this?" It would take me decades, well into my adulthood, to understand how my parents' relationship had affected my childhood and, ultimately, my future relationships.

One time, when I was around five, during one of the shared moments with my father, I felt safe enough to tell him about some of the "bad things" that were happening to me. On that particular night, I was up with a stomach ache, a relatively common event in my life. I was sitting on the little wooden potty chair in the pantry near the heating grate, straining to relieve the pain in my tummy. The chair held a plastic container that would slide into brackets on the bottom of the chair, right under the oval hole in the seat. My sister and I used this potty when we were very young, so that no one had to take us to the outhouse.

This particular evening, when I was done, my dad asked me with concern if I had eaten something that had made me sick. Intuitively I knew that food was not the cause of my distress.

Even at that tender age, I thought carefully before I responded. Dad had never punished me, not even with a small spanking, and I never saw him physically punish my siblings. Since my mother inflicted all of her punishments on us when my father was absent, I was not sure how he would react to what I wanted to say. Children who are abused do not easily or voluntarily offer such information about a parent. You come to believe that there is no one you can entirely trust in your life. I cautiously told my dad that my mother was "mean to me." I told him that when I was "bad," she would beat me with a belt and or have my brother force me into the cellar.

I prayed that he would grab me up in his big arms, tell me no one would ever hurt me again, and that he loved me more than anything in the world. Searching his face for a reaction, I saw no change in his expression. He stared blankly ahead, and as the silence continued, I wondered if he had been listening. The only motion in the room was his hand lifting his cigarette up to his mouth, and then down to the grate to flick the ashes. He opened his mouth to speak, and I just knew I was going to hear those words I had been waiting for so long. Instead, he told me it was time for me to go to bed. I swallowed my disappointment and did as I was told.

The next night, my father appeared at my bedside and told me to come downstairs. He did not need to wake me up because I was only pretending to be asleep. Earlier in the evening, I had heard my parents' angry, muffled voices coming from downstairs. Wanting to hear what was being said, I had quietly lifted the metal flue cover that was placed over the hole in the floor between my bedroom and the living room. I had lain on the floor, not breathing, waiting to hear if my father and mother were saying anything about me. I could not make out their words. My mother was using her scolding voice and my father's responses were angry. When I tired of listening, I got back into bed and tried unsuccessfully to go to sleep.

I followed my father downstairs as he had instructed me, and we sat on the heating grate, he on his chair, me on mine, like we did during our special times together. He blurted out that he was leaving the house, for he could no longer live with my mother. He told me I would never see him again. Panic invaded my body and took over head to toe. This was a time in my life when I held my father on a pedestal. I just knew that some day, when he was able to, he was going to rescue me. It did not matter that he was never around and that he did not protect me. He was my Hero Waiting to Happen, and he was all I had. And now he was leaving. He offered no additional explanation, and I asked for none. I did not have to. I knew exactly why he was going. I had caused this. He was leaving because I had told him about the "bad things."

My mother never came out of the bedroom during this entire episode. After my Dad had delivered his message, he told me to go back to bed. Empty and alone, I entered the dark, closed stairwell, sliding the palm of my hand along the wall as I pulled myself up the stairs. I heard the porch door slam. The engine of my father's pick-up truck started, a familiar sound to me. He took off down the road, leaving me, as he had done so many times before. Other times when I had heard these sounds, the thought would always enter my mind that he might never come back. This time he had actually told me he would not.

As was my father's pattern, he was back the next night. It had been the alcohol and his own deep pain talking. I was so thrilled when he returned that I vowed to myself not speak to him—or anyone else—about my struggles again. Not only did I keep my vow of silence for years, when my father was in the house I also pretended that everything was fine, so that he would not threaten to leave again. The tragic and ironic outcome of this event was that this little girl who desperately needed protection was now trying to protect her father.

My mother never spoke directly to me about what had happened, yet I knew that another shift had taken place in our house. My father had displayed directly both to her and to me his weakness and his inability to protect me. She was now fully in charge, and I was fully aware of that. I became angrier and angrier, at both of them. The trauma of this further abandonment by my father affected me for years to come.

⤳ COLD INSIDE AND OUT ⤴

Casselton is a small town that was ten miles west of the farm. It is where we attended Mass every Sunday, where my mother did the grocery shopping, and where the butcher shop was located. We raised beef livestock on our farm, mostly for sale, with two or three of the cattle kept for our personal consumption. When the annual sale of the herd took place, the cattle designated for our family was dressed at the butcher shop and stored in their large cold storage walk-in freezer facility. We kept a smaller stockpile of meat in the freezer on our porch, and when we ran out my father or mother would go to the butcher shop and bring home a new supply.

When I was six or seven years old, my brother and I went with our father to Casselton to pick up meat at the cold storage facility. My father told the butcher which cuts he wanted to take home, and then he left us in the shop to wait while he visited the dealer who sold farm machinery. My brother became bored sitting around, and to amuse himself he dared me to sneak into the walk-in freezer the next time the butcher opened the door. I thought about his idea for a few minutes. I was desperately seeking my brother's attention at this time in my life, so it seemed like an opportunity to gain his approval. I asked my brother how cold it would be in the freezer, and he assured me I did not have to stay in there that long. All I had to do was go in, look around and come out and tell him what I saw. My desire to impress my brother overrode any good sense I may have had.

I sat in the lobby of the shop and watched as the door to the large walk-in freezer room opened. The butcher came out with his hands and arms full of various cuts of meat, each wrapped in white waxed paper, the freezing cold air rushing out of the open door and flowing off his white coat as he carried the meat into the back area of the shop. Gathering up my courage, I seized the opportunity and charged into the cold storage freezer while the door was still partway open. Two frightening events happened next. I ran headfirst into the carcass of a frozen bull hanging from a big metal hook attached to a chain bolted to the ceiling, and then I heard the door to the freezer slam shut behind me.

I was stunned and scared. I looked around at the blood-red, skinned animals swaying in the freezing breeze created by the enormous cooling system. I turned around, looked at the closed door, and noticed that its glass window was coated with frost. I started shaking, from both the bitter cold and the overwhelming fear that was setting in.

I ran to the door and tried to open it by pushing down on the large handle. It did not budge. Either it was stuck or I did not have the strength to move it. Then I started to beat on the window. I tried to scrape off the heavy frost, but it was too thick and too hardened on the glass. I screamed as loudly as I could, "Please, someone let me out!" My pleading was drowned out by the howling sounds coming from the blower vents. I could not hear my own voice, yet I could see my words taking shape in the frozen breath coming out of my mouth. I beat on the window and screamed until I was exhausted by the cold and my panic. It was early summer, and I was not dressed to withstand an extended period in a commercial freezer, so I sat down on the floor and waited to freeze to death.

The next thing I remember was one of the butchers opening the door, with my brother beside him. The man lifted me up and took me into the warmest part of the shop. He sat me in a chair, put a blanket over me, and asked, "Are you going to be all right?" I nodded my head yes. It took several minutes for me to stop shivering and to return to full consciousness. My brother was standing by me, and he could see the terror on my face. When the butcher left the room, he whispered, "I closed the door after you went in, just to scare you a little, and I was going to open it in a minute or two. When I tried to lift the handle, I couldn't get the latch open, so I got the butcher and told him you'd gone into the freezer and the door closed behind you." Then he warned me, "Don't tell Dad what happened or we'll both get in trouble!" Although this logic makes no sense to me today, at the time I believed him. I was just glad to be alive.

I realize now that spending a little time locked in a cold storage freezer would not have been that unusual in my world. Long before this incident, I accepted the fact that being cold was a part of my life. North Dakota was bitterly cold. Our house was freezing cold. The underground cellar was always cold. My family was emotionally cold. And the freezer, like the cellar, represented a place of abandonment and isolation.

☙ TARGET PRACTICE ❧

When I was a child, my mother styled my hair with pink rubber curlers. She would wrap my wet hair around flexible rods that she then closed with a rubber latch attached to the curler. When my hair was dry, my mother would remove the curlers. Instead of combing my hair out, she would leave the curls in ringlets. Many little girls wore their hair this way. It was an easy styling technique for a parent, and at the time I thought it made me look cute.

I'm telling you about the curlers because my head happened to be covered with them the day of target practice. My brother and his friend from a nearby farm were playing by the barn. I was eight years old and, as I said, always trying to get my brother to pay attention to me, so I went over to the boys to see what they were doing. I knew that my brother did not want his little sister hanging around, especially when he had a friend over, yet I kept trying to be one of the gang. I pestered the two of them long enough that they finally made me part of their next game. My brother and his friend decided to place me in front of a stack of hay bales and use me as a target for bow and arrow practice. Actually, I was to be a reverse target, since the object was to have their arrows hit as close to me as possible without striking me. They both assured me that they were good archers, and that they would not aim directly at me. My desire to be included overrode any fears I may have had about the activity.

I stood in front of the hay bales, and the first arrow whizzed by my head. One of the boys shouted out, "That was close!" The next arrow pinned me to the hay bales as it went between my scalp and the pink curlers. This time the boys did not shout anything. They watched in silence as I passed out.

I think about this today, taking deep breaths, and am amazed I was not killed. That would have been a horrible outcome, obviously for me, but also for my brother. He was spared the guilt of killing me or causing serious physical injury. Yet I internalized the terror I felt from this experience for a very, very long time. And to me, *my brother's act was one that I felt I could never forgive.* The freezer episode had been terrifying, but the target practice was evil.

❧ THE RACE ❦

One day, when I was nine or ten, my brother challenged my younger sister and me to a race to the artesian well where the cattle and sheep watered. I remember that there was to be a prize for the winner, more than likely having the losers do his or her chores. I had raced my brother and sister on this path many times before, and my brother, being the oldest and fastest, always won. I kept racing though, always hoping that someday I would win. This race was different.

The well was in the livestock pasture, about 200 yards from the house. To get to the well, we would have to run between the barn and the pig pen. We started the race outside the wooden fence in front of the house, and my brother took the lead. I ran as fast as I could, and I was surprised when I actually caught up to him. Soon I had the lead, and it looked like this time I was going to win.

I did not see the line of barbed wire that had been strung between the barn and the pig pen, and I ran right into it. The barbed wire caught me under my right eye and knocked me to the ground. Had I not been running with my chin up, I would have been blinded. Blood poured down my face from the wound under my eye. I remember my brother running over and staring down at me. His look of curiosity was tinged with shock. My sister started screaming when she saw the blood and ran to the house. Once again, I left my body to cope with the terror. This was not a conscious decision on my part; it seemed to "just happen." It was a survival technique I had developed as a very young girl, and throughout my childhood this reaction became automatic when I felt in grave danger.

That night when my father got home, he saw the bandage that my mother had applied under my eye. When my mother told him what had happened, he started yelling. I was surprised since he had never shown such a direct display of anger when we children were present. When he got upset with one of us kids, the standard punishment was "the look." He would get quiet, although the anger was there on his face.

This time he was furious. He demanded to know why "the race" had been held when both my mother and my brother knew he had put up the barbed wire fence that morning. There was silence at the table. He was looking at my brother, and my brother was staring back at him. My mother continued eating. After a short silence, my father went back to his dinner.

I was very quiet during the meal, knowing that if I offered any comments, I would pay the price for it later. My brother and I had had several prior discussions about what happened to tattletales. A part of me wanted to scream out how scared and mad I was, and I felt myself holding back tears. At the same time, I was thinking about what would happen if I said anything. My father might yell at my brother. My mother would probably say nothing. And my brother would retaliate when he was alone with me. So I kept my mouth shut one more time in a series of many similar silences.

After he finished his meal, my father went into his and my mother's bedroom and changed out of his OshKosh B'Gosh overalls into his "town clothes." He got in his pickup truck and sped off to his favorite bar in Mapleton. Hope failed me one more time as my "white knight" left again.

Years later I found out about the childhood accident in which my father had lost one of his eyes. The possibility of my encountering the same fate must have brought his own painful memories back to the surface. As was his policy with regard to his behavior, he contained any pain or anger he experienced at the dinner table that evening until he could get to the bar to dull it with alcohol.

Today, I tenderly put my makeup on that scar and am grateful that I did not lose my vision that day. Instead I am grateful that I obtained a valuable insight. I could no longer hold out any hope that my father was going to help me, and my brother was no longer my friend or protector. He had become my tormentor.

❧ THE WINDS OF CHANGE ❧

For years, my brother had been my hero. When I was very little, I looked up to him as my protector. He would pull me to my feet if I took a tumble, or he would scare away the farm animals if they got too close to me. He had a sheepish grin and with it he could bring me out of tears and into laughter.

Our relationship during the first two years of my life is portrayed perfectly in the photographs my mother took of us during this period. When I am three months old and my brother is three, we both sit on the front step of our house, and he has his arms around me, holding on for dear life. At ten months old, I am dressed in a blue snowsuit, sitting in front of him on a sled, and again he has his arms tightly wrapped around my waist. As a four-and-a-half-year-old, he is grabbing my eighteen-month- old shoulders to make sure I do not fall down while our picture is being taken with our red wagon outside our house. A month later, a picture shows him holding my hand so I do not fall on the cement sidewalk in front of my great aunt's house. I trusted him, for we had an unspoken common bond. We both knew about pain, and we both knew about hurt. I watched my brother suffer severe punishments, and it caused me tremendous emotional pain. And when I was abused, I could also see the hurt on his little face.

I was my brother's buddy, and I idolized him. My brother was eight and I was five when my sister turned three. This is when I noticed that he started paying less attention to me and began focusing his protective behavior on her. By this time, he had become more and more withdrawn, and he was spending less time around the house. He seemed to be mad all the time, and then he started to take out his anger on me. I did not understand what was changing, and I felt like he had abandoned me.

I did not blame him for following my mother's instructions and standing on the cellar door to lock me in. I knew what would happen to him or to my sister, whom my mother also sometimes instructed to do this, if they disobeyed her. But my brother's deliberate cruelty—locking me in the freezer, using me for target practice, tricking me into running into the barbed wire fence—were his acts and his alone.

None of what was happening made any sense to me at the time. All I knew for sure was that I felt betrayed by everyone, including my brother. My hero had become my attacker; he was now one more person in my family I could not trust.

❧ THE JUNKYARD DOG ❦

I know what it is like to be a stray dog, hungry and scavenging for food. You feel free when you are roaming the fields and meadows, but never safe when you are confined in a hostile environment. It is very unsettling for a child to have parents who vacillate between neglecting and abusing you. Your world is unsafe, you feel invisible, unimportant.

I often felt like that. But there was also that other element in my personality, the part of me that my mother called "willful" and that looking back, I see as being responsible for my survival. Whether I was born with this trait or I developed it, I was the independent child in our family and the challenging one. I was also the adventurous one.

The farm had many old buildings that had been abandoned and left for nature to consume. We kids had all been instructed not to go into these structures, as they were on the verge of collapse. When my brother turned seven or eight, my father would take him out into the fields to help with chores. My younger sister was the baby, so most of the time she stayed in the house with my mother. I observed little of the interaction between them because I preferred not to be in the house. After school and on weekends, left on my own as I often was, I ignored the rule and would roam the farm and the surrounding area to explore the dark and dangerous buildings, looking for lost treasures and excitement.

No one seemed to mind my absence, and no one came looking for me. Sometimes when I came back to the house, the back porch screen door and the front door would be locked. This was a sign that my mother was busy with housework or tending to my sister, or that she was napping, and did not want to be disturbed. I would sit and wait and daydream, until the hook was unlatched and I was allowed to go into the house. Sometimes I would spend the whole day playing outside and exploring the farm, causing me to burn up a lot of energy and get very hungry. I would hear the familiar growling sound in my stomach and feel a gnawing sensation, and I would rush home to eat. If I had missed the assigned lunch hour, my mother made me wait until dinner to eat. If I did not think I could make it until then, I would take a trip to the junkyard to find scraps of food in the garbage that had been dumped there.

The junkyard was one of the places on the off-limits list. It was located at the edge of the farm, next to the train tracks and close to an abandoned grain elevator. The huge yard was the repository for anything that needed to be disposed of on the farm. The ground was piled high with old farm machinery parts, bald tires, discarded stoves and refrigerators, broken furniture, batteries, oil drums, paint cans, railroad ties and many other forms of debris. It was a dangerous place since it was adjacent to an active railroad track, and the hobos riding the rails tended to jump off at the junkyard looking for food and shelter. It was also a haven for rats and various other vermin. It smelled of rotting food, burned rubber, and decaying animals.

Even with all its dangers, I would search the junkyard looking for something edible. I remember what a thrill it was to find an old catsup bottle with a small amount of catsup remaining on the bottom. I would turn the bottle upside down and wait for the contents to flow down so I could reach in with my small finger, get some on my fingertip, and lick it up.

I liked roaming the fields and the woods because I loved being by myself. Even if it meant avoiding the junkyard rats and battling the outdoor elements, instinctively I felt safer when I was alone.

❧ THE BUNNY HUTCH ❧

As a ten-year-old girl, I painstakingly built a hutch in which to raise rabbits. Constructing the hutch was a difficult project. Raising rabbits was not.

One of the buildings between the main farm buildings and the railroad tracks was so dilapidated that our family never used it during the time we lived on the farm. The landlord had built it as a boarding house for the hired men who worked the fields before we took over managing the farm as sharecroppers. When the building became totally unstable, my father and uncle used a tractor with a hydraulic lift attached to the front of it to demolish the old structure by forcing the walls to cave in and the roof to collapse. I would often visit the demolished building when I was on one of my adventures, as it provided a new and dangerous place to explore. It also provided me the scrap wood I needed to build a home for my rabbits in the backyard area between the porch and the outhouse.

I picked out two-by-fours to make the frame and nailed these pieces together using a hammer and nails I borrowed from the tool shed. I constructed the sides of the two-foot-high cage from laths—narrow strips of wood—that I also gathered from the old building. I attached these to the frame, leaving a two-inch space between each piece. I left the top of the hutch open. It was not extremely sturdy and it tilted to one side, yet it served the purpose, and I was proud of it.

It was summertime, and I managed to capture a couple of rabbits by throwing a blanket over them when I found them nibbling on our cabbage and carrots in the backyard garden. As tenderly as I could, I placed them in their new mansion. I picked vegetables from the garden for them or fed them vegetable scraps left over from our meals. I found an old pie pan at the junkyard to use as a watering dish. I made sure it was always full, and I visited my rabbits every day.

I had no idea what sex the pair was since I did not comprehend the concept of different genders in rabbits. Obviously I had caught a boy rabbit and a girl rabbit, for soon I had five little bunnies in the hutch. I never thought about how they got there, and no one offered any explanation. It made no difference to me; I only cared that now I had my own family to care for.

One day I was outside feeding my furry friends when my brother came over to me at their cage. He had never shown any interest in my domesticated pets, as he preferred the field-roaming rabbits he could hunt with his rifle. I noticed he had an angry look on his face, and I wondered if he had gotten into trouble with my mother or if my father had criticized him for how he had performed his chores in the field. My brother took hold of the sides of the cage, making them wobble back and forth, and I knew he was trying to get a rise out of me. The hutch had become more fragile with time, and his moving the sides like this loosened the nails and made them start to come out. I shouted at him to stop or he was going to break the cage. He sneered at me and shook it harder.

When I saw he wasn't going to stop shaking it, I charged at him and hit him with my body, full force. I caught him off guard and knocked him to the ground. He got a stunned look on his face, shocked by the fact that I could inflict such a blow to him. He did not say a word as he stood up. He gave me a dirty look, pushed me down to the ground, and stomped into the house. I could tell that he was mad, and I felt that he was also embarrassed that his little sister had tackled him.

I picked myself up and walked over to the hutch. I was proud of myself, for I had protected my little family.

I reached into the cage to try to pet the bunnies. They were accustomed to my picking them up and stroking them, and usually they enjoyed it. This time they ran to the corners of the cage, their little bodies shivering in fright from the recent attack on their home. I heard the porch door slam, and I looked up to see my brother approaching with his rifle. I stood up and froze in place, eyeing the gun and not sure what was going to happen next.

My brother stood over the cage, took aim, and shot the heads off of each of my rabbits one by one. The sight of the red blood running down their white and brown fur was horrific. The last thing I remember noticing was the mother rabbit's black eyeballs darting from side to side before her head left her body. No cries came from my little pets, for death came quickly. The only sounds in the air were the shots coming from the gun my brother had received as a Christmas present. When he was done, my brother turned and walked away without saying a word.

For what seemed liked eternity, I could not bring my voice to speak or my body to move. No one came to investigate the shots or what had happened. Eventually, I walked into the house and went upstairs to my room, and I sobbed and sobbed. Hours later I came downstairs and forced myself go outside. Someone had cleaned up the massacre in the yard. The body parts were gone and the broken pieces of the cage were in the old rusty barrel that we used to burn our garbage. No one ever discussed this event or asked what happened to my rabbit family.

I will never forget the anger, terror, and sadness I felt at that time. The anger was focused on my brother, for he had raised the bar on cruelty to a whole new level.

❧ GRANDMA'S HOUSE ❧

When I was growing up, Grandma Serum, my mother's mother, lived in the same farmhouse on the family homestead in Minnesota that her late husband Oliver had brought her to so many years before. It was about an hour's drive away from our farm. My uncle Almont, my mother's brother, farmed the property. He lived with my Grandma, as he had never married. My mother's sisters—my aunts Iola, Virginia, and Ardale—all lived a short drive away.

From the time I was four years old until my grandmother got sick, when I was about eight, I would spend the summer with her on her farm. Her house was very large compared to ours and it had a porch running the entire length of the back of the house. It also had a piano, which I loved and where I used to spend a lot of time plunking around. It had an indoor bathroom and an attic full of fascinating things for me to explore.

In the basement was a very large wrought-iron coal-burning cooking stove. Grandma would open the grill on the front of the stove to shovel in coal and light the fire. On top of the stove were six iron disks, which functioned as burners. About an hour after lighting the coals, she would push a curved steel handle into the slot at the side of a disk, and while raising the hot disk she would jostle the coals with a poker to keep them burning. Grandma used to bake me crumb cake (a rolled up thin cookie) in the oven of that stove, and she would fry lefse (a Norwegian potato pancake) directly on a hot disk. When the lefse started to turn brown, she would use a spatula to carefully lift it off the stove, and we then put butter and sugar on it. Sharing lefse with my grandmother, I thought I was in heaven.

Grandma took care of the house, the cooking, the laundry, and the chickens. Every day, she and I would go out and pick the eggs in the chicken coop. She had names for most of the hens. We brought the eggs into the kitchen, where we would wash each one, and then pack them in egg crates so that my uncle Almont could take them to town to sell them. I broke quite a few eggs in the process, but it didn't seem to bother Grandma. My uncle, whom I loved dearly, did comment that we ate a lot more scrambled eggs when I was around.

Grandma was always busy, so during the summers I visited her I spent most of my time on her back porch. I had imaginary friends, imaginary parties, imaginary dances, and imaginary plays. I also created a lot of poetry in my head. That porch was my playhouse, my studio, and my stage. I would have slept out there if she would have let me.

That farmhouse was the safest place in the world to me. Grandma never punished me, and I remember only a few times when she raised her voice. She was a very silent person, saying little even when she asked me to sit by her. Often I would catch her looking at me, and sometimes it seemed as if she was ready to ask me something. She never did, other than to tell me I was kind of scrawny. She certainly fed me well when I was staying with her.

At the end of my first summer with Grandma, when it was time to go back home, I threw a tantrum. I slid under my grandmother's old pedal-driven sewing machine to try to hide. As my aunt Iola dragged me out by my legs, I started screaming. I still have that picture in my head today.

The second summer I stayed with my grandmother I was five years old. By then I had stopped wondering why no one ever asked me why I didn't want to go home at the end of the summer. Although I was too young to put it into words, I now fully understood that not asking and not telling were part of the rules in my family.

As I mentioned earlier, my mother's father had died when my mother was a toddler, leaving my Grandma to raise five children by herself and manage the farm. As much as I adored her, I now wonder what kind of mother Grandma had been. Did the stress of having responsibility for the family and the farm bring out the worst in her? Was her protection and loving care of me some sort of repayment for her own behavior toward my mother and her other children? I will never know, so I am left to wonder.

My precious Grandma died when I was ten years old. I did not understand what death was, and it was never explained to me. All I knew was that I never saw her again.

❧ THE INVISIBLE RELATIVES ❧

My father's brother Bernard and his family lived on the same farmstead as us, in a house twice the size of ours and 100 feet from our yard. Like my father, Uncle Bernard was a sharecropper. He and my dad were partners and divided the farming duties between them. They worked hard, yelled at each other, laughed together, and cussed a lot. The two of them were more like twins than mere siblings, and it was clear that they loved each other very much.

I ran into my uncle on occasion when I was out exploring the farm or roaming about. He was always kind to me, although he regularly scolded me for being someplace he did not think I should be, like the junkyard. He said he was concerned that I might hurt myself. You could always tell where my uncle was on the farm, for he swore louder and with more passion than anybody. I had to write down what he said and later ask my brother what it meant. It usually had something to do with farm animals and sexual activities, and my brother told me never to say those words. I liked my uncle because he was nice to me, and especially since my dad seemed to care for him so much.

My uncle lived in the "big house" with my aunt, my four girl cousins and one boy cousin. When we were children, my mother instructed my brother, sister, and me that we were not allowed to play with our cousins (who were in the same age range as us) or to go into their yard or to enter their house (which was in very close proximity). She told us "their family has their own house and we have ours, and everybody needs to stay on their own side." There was a massive oak tree in the yard between our houses, and it established the line of demarcation that we could not cross. During the spring and summer months, dense foliage on the oak tree partially blocked our view of the big house. Autumn brought a mass of fallen leaves under the tree, and a complete view of our relatives' residence just across the yard.

My mother gave us this directive not to socialize when my brother was five and I was two. My brother remembers her giving us this instruction, although I do not. On the other hand, I certainly remember knowing that I was not to socialize with them. Our families never shared holidays or celebrations together, and, although we went to the same church, the two families attended Mass at different times, so we did not encounter each other there. As close as my father and his brother were, and despite their working the farm together six days a week, I never remember seeing my uncle in our house.

My uncle had the same dark brown eyes and black hair as my dad, and they were both clean shaven. My uncle smoked constantly, even when he was caring for the barn and the dairy cattle. One of his daily jobs was milking the cows. Occasionally I went with him into the pasture to round them up and bring them into the barn. I watched in fascination as he silently performed his milking chores. He had a humorous, affectionate attitude toward the animals, and he had given names to his favorites. At times I would walk into the barn as he stood there with the aluminum milk pail, saying "Bossy, get into your stall" or "Keep that tail to yourself, Blacky."

Uncle Bernard's children spent their free time playing in their house or yard, and they almost never came into the milking barn with their father. Since he was alone with the cows most of the time, I think he enjoyed having my company. He allowed me to sit by him on a wooden stool, and when I got a little older he taught me how to milk the cows. At first I was frightened by their size. I had seen the cows swish their heavy tails at the black flies that annoyed them and kick their strong hind legs at the barnyard cats who tried to get into the milk bucket. But my uncle explained to me that the cows actually enjoy being milked, for it relieves the pressure in their udders. I liked that explanation, since it seemed like he was doing a nice thing for them and, in turn, they were giving us milk to drink.

After I finally got the hang of the milking procedure, I made a point of stopping by the barn. I would sit on the stool next to my uncle and wait for him to give me some news about the cows, whether one of them was going to have a baby or was not feeling well. Often we sat silently, listening to the rhythmic sounds of the milk streams as they hit the sides and bottom of the pail. This reminded me of the way I sat silently on the grate with my father, listening to the sounds of the furnace.

My aunt spent most of her time in their home, attending to the household affairs and her children, so I had little contact with her. She was tall and thin, had rimless glasses, and always wore a dress. She smiled a lot and had a pleasant laugh.

In the yard between the two houses, each family had its own large vegetable garden with rows and rows of tomatoes, cucumbers, lettuce, cabbage, radishes, corn, potatoes, peas, and beans. My father and my uncle had hammered wooden stakes into the ground at the end of the rows, attaching an empty seed packet to each stake to identify what had been had planted in that row. The two gardens were side by side, with a two-foot high metal fence separating the plantings.

Occasionally, when I was in our garden picking some vegetables my mother had requested for a meal, my aunt would also be in her garden. She would look over at me and say hello. Keeping her head and shoulders bent over the row she was harvesting, she would ask me, "How was your day today?" I would relay some playtime or school event to her, peeking over at my house to see if my mother was outside watching. Although I hadn't been told I could not speak to my aunt, somehow I knew that if I was not allowed into her house, I was also not allowed to talk to her. When I finished my chores, I went back to our house, my vegetables in hand and my secret conversation in my head.

My oldest cousin was four years older than my brother. She spent most of her time in her house helping my aunt with chores and caring for some of her younger siblings. The three younger girl cousins and my boy cousin played in the house a lot, although occasionally I watched them playing on their swing set in their part of the yard or in the sandbox their father had made out of a discarded John Deere tractor tire. If I sat backwards on one of the swings on our swing set, and they were swinging on their swings, I would be facing them and we could swing in unison as we watched each other. My girl cousins almost always wore dresses, even to play in. Although I did not talk to them, seeing them in dresses gave me the idea that, since I was a girl, I should be wearing a dress too. I did not understand my mother's insistence that I should wear my brother's hand-me-down pants and overalls and be grateful for them.

My boy cousin was the youngest of the tribe, and, until he started going to school, he was generally in the house with my aunt. As I have said, my brother began going into the fields with my dad when he was seven or eight years old. When our cousin reached this age, he did not do farm chores with my Uncle Bernard. Either he had no interest or his parents did not want him to do so. I never encountered any of my cousins while I roamed the farm and its environs, nor did I expect to. I had come to realize that I was the "wild child" in the bunch.

All of the cousins went to the same elementary school. One of the girl cousins was in my brother's grade and one was in my grade. Every school day morning, the two separate groups of children left their respective homes to walk to the spot where the bus picked us up for school. While we stood waiting for the bus to arrive, conversations took place between my brother and one of the older girl cousins about an upcoming event at school or, after we got a television set, about a program they had seen the night before. My cousin and I who were in the same grade talked about a teacher, a homework assignment or a school project. One day while we were waiting for the bus, my oldest girl cousin told us that their mother had informed them that they were not welcome in our house. That cleared up at least one mystery - why they never attempted to visit us.

None of us had been explicitly told that we could not associate with our cousins at school, so we maintained a friendly attitude toward each other while we were there. But although we played together at school in group activities, we never reached out to one another as family. We did not invest time getting close to each other at school since those friendships were impossible outside of that environment. As genetics played out, most of my cousins bore a strong resemblance to their mother as we did to the maternal side of our family. Since we did not look at all like our cousins, very seldom did anyone at school mistake us for siblings even though all of us had the same last name. The teachers and students knew we were related and lived on the same farm, yet no one was aware that we did none of the things together that children living on the same farm would normally do, such as homework or playing inside or outside each other's houses.

At the time, my brother, sister, and I did not talk about this situation among ourselves, nor did we ever discuss it with my cousins. No one challenged the instructions we had been given, or questioned the logic or reasoning behind them. So as odd as these circumstances now appear, looking through adult eyes, this was a perfectly normal situation to me as a child.

As an older teenager, I started attending my cousins' birthday parties at their house. It was strange to walk into their home for the first time after so many years of steering clear of it. The house had a lot more space than ours, with a large kitchen and several bedrooms. Perhaps it was the size that made it feel more open and friendly, or maybe it was the lighter energy of the occupants.

It is still a mystery to me today as to why this separation between the families happened. I wondered about it off and on for years as an adult, yet none of my family members were willing to discuss it except for my brother. He believes it stemmed from the fact that our family was relegated to the converted train depot while my uncle's family got the bigger home, and there was envy involved. I believe there was an unresolved issue between my mother and my aunt, who once said she could not understand why my mother did not like her. Whatever happened, it affected our lives for the entire 25 years the families lived together on the farm. This separation added one more layer of isolation to my already insular world.

The reason for the lifelong feud no longer matters, but the lifelong effects are significant. The separation between the families was a tragedy for all of us, especially the children. Years of possible friendships, shared playtime, and companionship were lost, for reasons long ago forgotten and that never should have impinged on our lives to begin with. We children became pawns in an ugly adult chess game. Children really do pay for the sins of their parents.

I learned a lot about distance on the farm. Not the mile we had to walk to the mailbox or the 100 yards to the barn, but about emotional distance. I learned that you can live within a stone's throw of your nearest extended family and have almost no idea what their lives are like or who they really are. You can live in the same house as your parents and siblings and, hard as you try, have no emotional or spiritual bond with any of them. I learned that when somebody or something does not work out in your life, all you had to do was distance yourself from it.

I thought this technique was working for me until well into adulthood when I discovered that there are not enough miles on earth to fully distance yourself from your past trauma and your pain.

◈ SUMMER VISITORS ◈

Shortly before my parents' marriage, my father's mother, Blanche, had moved to California with some of her younger children. When I was growing up, my Aunt Bertha still lived in California, near her mother, but my Aunt Lorine had moved to Hawaii. Occasionally, my aunts traveled together to visit us on the farm during their summer vacations. They brought their children along, and having all of them around was one of the few happy family events I remember from my childhood.

I think Bertha was my father's favorite sister. They had the same wry sense of humor, and she told wicked jokes and smoked two packs of cigarettes a day just like he did. By the time I knew her, the nicotine was already starting to take its toll on her lungs, resulting in a laugh that was hoarse and throaty. Bertha's son and daughter, my cousins, were the loves of her life, and she relished bringing them to see us so we could get to know each other.

Everyone called Lorine by her nickname, Tuty. She was a striking, flamboyant woman, and an artist. She wore brightly-colored dresses, long dangling earrings, and jewelry made out of seashells and beads. She also wore make-up and bright red lipstick. Whenever her daughter or one of her sons came close to her, she would almost always give them a hug or kiss. Aunt Tuty did not act like or look like any of the farm wives I was accustomed to seeing. There was an instant connection between Tuty and me, and I knew that she loved me.

My aunts were kind to everyone, and they were very affectionate. They were always hugging and kissing me, and at first I did not know what to think. That was very foreign to me. They both smelled of sweet perfume, and I would wind up with red lipstick all over my face when they were done. They were both very strong women who held their own with anybody. I scarcely believed it when they told me it was perfectly fine to be married and to take trips without your husband. The men they had married adored them and worshipped the ground on which they traveled, also a foreign concept in my world. What I liked most about my aunts was the adoration they displayed for their children. They planted the seeds for the possibility of a very different type of life for me in the future.

One summer, on the morning my aunts and their children were scheduled to arrive, my mother had woken me and discovered that I had wet the bed. This was a recurring event in my childhood, and by this time in my life my mother thought I should have outgrown this "problem." With her face screwed up in a look of disgust, her finger wagging at me, she said "You can just stay there and think about what you did. Little girls that can't control themselves can lie in their own pee." She then let me know that she had just washed the sheets and that they were not going to be changed again. This was the punishment she usually administered if I wet the bed, which sometimes happened because I would have bad nightmares and did not make it to the bathroom in time. My mother's concept seemed to be that if I lay in my own urine long enough, I would cease this behavior. This turned out to be an ineffective technique. Indeed, its only effect was to add another level of embarrassment to my life and to further deplete my sense of self value. The morning my aunts and cousins arrived, my mother forbade me to come out of my bedroom.

My mother told Lorine that I was being disciplined and that I was to stay in my room. My aunt, having traveled all the way from Hawaii to see me, was going to have none of that. She marched up the stairs, opened the door, and approached my bed. I had pulled the blankets over my head. She drew the covers back and saw that I was curled up, sucking my thumb, and soaked in my own urine. I will never forget the look on her face. Her eyes opened wide, and I was not sure if she was going to cry or scream. I was twelve years old when my aunt found me hiding under the blankets, wet with urine. I could barely look at her. The years of my mother and brother abusing me, my father abandoning me by failing to protect me, both my parents neglecting me, and the isolation I experienced on the farm had all taken its toll. Even though my strong will and independent nature had kept me alive, I was still a child, and the circumstances of my life had extracted a terrible price from me. I felt invisible, worthless, unlovable, and dirty. Little girls like me should lie in a pool of urine.

Lorine hugged me for the longest time, and then cleaned me up and took me downstairs. She was like an angel to me. Unfortunately, during that visit, my aunts had a horrific fight with my father's brother, Bernard. The argument started because one of the boy cousins kissed the cheek of one of the girl cousins at a movie we all attended the evening before. When my uncle heard that one of his sisters' sons had kissed his daughter, he became enraged and demanded that his sisters and their children leave the farm immediately. I found out about all of this the next morning, when my Dad woke me up and told me to come and say goodbye to my aunts because they were leaving. I remember starting to cry and beating on him with my fists, something I would normally never do. I screamed, "Everything always gets ruined on this farm." His response was not to respond, just to walk out of my room.

I got dressed quickly and rushed out of the house. My father was already in his car, with my aunts in the backseat. I heard him telling my mother he was going to drive his sisters into the field so they could say goodbye to their brother. I forced myself into the backseat of the car before he could object and sat next to my Aunt Bertha. When we got to the field where my uncle was plowing, Bernard refused to talk to his sisters or even stop his tractor long enough for them to approach. I remember they tried to get his attention by screaming at him, or, more accurately, screaming at the back of the tractor.

They shouted that they did not know what they had done wrong. My Aunt Bertha was sobbing, and even through her wailing I heard her tell my uncle that she loved him. I saw that my Aunt Tuty was shaken by what was happening, but her tightly compressed lips also revealed her anger. My father did not intervene between his brother and his sisters. I watched as he did nothing to alter the chain of events. My uncle was very stubborn, and very caught up in his anger, and I knew my father was trying to "keep the peace" with someone he worked with every day of his life.

We drove back to my uncle's house, where my aunts and cousins had been staying, a one-mile trip that seemed to last for eternity. No words were spoken, and my aunts could not control their crying. Their pain was so intense that I felt pained for them. But I was thinking more about my life on that farm. Normally, the abuse, abandonment, and isolation were meted out on separate occasions; this event was a grand triple play. My beloved aunts were callously discarded by my uncle, and I witnessed that abuse. My father had abandoned me by not intervening in this dreadful situation. And with the dispatching of the relatives I adored, my life became even further isolated. My relationship with my Uncle Bernard was never again as friendly.

When we got back to the house, my aunts gathered up my five cousins, and my father drove them into Fargo, where they stayed in a hotel until they caught a flight back to California. My aunts and my cousins were never allowed to come back to the farm again. As I watched my father drive them down the dusty dirt road, I did not cry, for by that time I had used up most of my allotment of childhood tears. Before this event, I used to cry when I was frightened or sad. After my aunts left, I still had all of those feelings, but I no longer expressed them with tears.

In spite of this event, both my aunts remained an important part of my life throughout my young adulthood. Many years later, my Aunt Lorine surprised me by coming to my wedding in Minneapolis. She brought me a bouquet of live anthuriums, which she had carried in her arms for twelve hours on three separate planes so that they would not get damaged. Her gesture symbolized the love and protection that she had tried to bring into my life since I was a child.

❧ BEVERLY ❧

Television gave me a magical glimpse into the lives of families very different from mine—ones that I was convinced were make-believe. Much to my amazement, I discovered a real life family very much like the television families. As fate would have it, this family befriended me, and provided a precious thread of joy that was woven throughout my childhood, and that helped me survive the conditions of my family life.

We did not own a television set until I was six years old. This contributed to the fact that I knew very little about how people outside of our farm conducted their lives. As a young child, my attendance at the obligatory Sunday Mass at St. Leo's Parish in Casselton gave me one of my few opportunities to study other families. In this pastoral environment, I observed that everyone behaved similarly to how my family acted when we were in public. Parents were friendly and after Mass they stopped on the church steps to talk to each other about farming or the upcoming weather. Children were expected to be quiet, to smile, and always to be polite when responding to adults. Nothing in these encounters led me to think that our family was not identical to all other families.

I knew that other families owned television sets, however, as I overheard some of the children in kindergarten talking about them. Also, my brother would come home from school telling us that all his friends had TVs. He talked incessantly about "Roy Rogers" and "Howdy Doody," which he had learned about at school. He bugged my father for months about buying one. I expressed only marginal interest in the idea of us owning a TV, since I assumed we would never be able to afford such a luxury in our house. Therefore, I was more surprised than excited when my father brought one home when I was six years old. I wondered where the money had come from to purchase something as expensive as a television set when I was wearing hand-me-down boy's clothes to school. I tucked that thought away for future consideration and decided to focus on the new acquisition my father was taking out of the huge box.

The 1950s television sets were housed in a large, wooden console cabinet. Our TV was a light pecan color, and it doubled as a piece of furniture on which my mother's collectibles were displayed. During the process of setting up the television, my father hooked up a rabbit ear antenna that he placed on top of it to capture the signal being transmitted from twenty miles away in Fargo. The reception this flimsy contraption provided was not very good, so a few days later Dad brought home an outside antenna, which he and my uncle installed on the roof. Even with this more powerful receiver, reception in the countryside was not great. Fortunately, we did not realize this at the time. The snowy figures looked very natural to us. And although the console was big, the actual TV screen was very small, so we kids would sit on the floor, with our faces almost touching the glass.

I would watch "Father Knows Best," "Leave It to Beaver,"

"Ozzie and Harriet," and "The Donna Reed Show." I assumed that these were all just made-up stories, for they did not represent life in my household. The fathers on these shows had professional jobs, they wore "dress-up" clothes all the time, and they came home from work every night right before dinner. When the Television Father opened the front door, he was greeted cheerfully by his wife and children. At the dinner table, all the family members held a lively discussion of the day's events. If any of the children had gotten into trouble that day, or had a problem needing attention, the parents would discuss the situation with the child and then have a conversation about the best course of action to be taken. The parents would decide whether a reprimand was needed, and if it was, they would come to a mutual decision on the appropriate punishment.

The Television Parents did not scream or yell, they were never drunk, they did not beat the children or lock them in a cellar, and the children were always at the center of attention in the family. No, I knew this could not be real life. Clearly, it was the product of someone's overly active imagination.

Then one day, I went to Beverly's house. I first met Beverly a year before we got a television, when she and I started kindergarten together at Mapleton elementary school. Beverly had an angelic face, and her blonde hair was styled with ringlets. Her curls were similar to mine, although more neatly arranged and held back with little barrettes. She wore a frilly, feminine dress and patent leather shoes almost every day. She was the prettiest girl, and she had the best singing voice. I could tell immediately that she was going to be the most popular person in class. The other girls wanted to be associated with her, and they surrounded her like they were attending to a queen. Even the boys, at this tender age, would tease her in an attempt to get her attention.

During recess, we were required to go outside onto the playground. I dreaded this part of the schedule, for it meant having to interact with the other children. By kindergarten age, I was very shy and withdrawn, so I did not make eye contact with most of the children. I avoided the merry-go-round and the teeter-totter, instead choosing the solo activity of swinging.

One day, our teacher, Mrs. Nordland, made an announcement to the class that sent panic throughout my body. She told us that during recess, all of us would be participating in a three-legged race. This terrified me, as it meant that I would have to engage in activity with another student. I also knew that no one would want to pair up with me, for I did not feel I was worthy of being selected. The humiliation of the upcoming rejection added to the panic I felt about the impending social interaction.

I waited solemnly on the side of the playground as the other children started to pair up. To my surprise, I saw little Beverly walking in my direction. When she stopped in front of me, she said in her sweet and kind voice, "Would you like to be my partner?" I looked up to see if the teacher was watching, for surely she had instructed Beverly to ask me. But Mrs. Nordlund was busy tying pairs of children's legs together. I looked around to see if there was a group of girls waiting to break into laughter when Beverly would yell out that she was "just kidding." I observed no such conspiratorial group. I looked at Beverly again, and, unable to speak, just nodded my head yes and stood in silence next to this lovely little girl.

The teacher made her rounds and ultimately came over to Beverly and me. I watched as Mrs. Nordlund tied my right leg to Beverly's left leg with a strip of cloth. Beverly's leg was beautifully bare as it came out from under the hem of her dress; my leg was covered by a ragged hand-me-down boy's pants. When Mrs. Nordlund finished tying our legs together, I finally had the courage to look again at the little girl to whom I was now attached. She was smiling at me, and there was an instant connection between us.

Beverly had run a three-legged race before and I had not.

When she suggested that we take our first step using the middle "leg," I deferred to her four-year-old wisdom in this matter. It took us less than a minute of practicing to develop our rhythm and technique. We won that first three-legged race in kindergarten and every subsequent race for years to come. The annual school picnic at Lindenwood Park gave us the chance to show off our talent in an even broader competition. There were always contenders trying to take our title away, yet that never happened. We reigned supreme. We became one runner and one spirit.

In contrast to us "farm kids," Beverly was one of the "town kids," as she lived in a house a few blocks away from the school. My mother forbade me to leave the school grounds to go into the town area (less than four blocks from the school) or into any of the houses of the town people. She said that the town kids did not have to work as hard as the farm kids and she let me know they were spoiled. My mother made it clear that she didn't want to catch me in one of their houses. In spite of this instruction, in second grade when Beverly asked me if I wanted to go home with her during the lunch period, I only hesitated for a moment. I had never been to the house of one of the "town people," and that potential adventure was worth any future punishment.

I could not believe my eyes when I walked through Beverly's front door for the first time. The house seemed gigantic. On the first floor was a very large kitchen, a sitting room for guests, another large living room (with a television) for the family, and the parents' bedroom. The bedrooms for Beverly, her two young brothers, and one younger sister were all upstairs. The house had a well-lit basement, complete with a light switch at the top of the stairwell. There were no bulbs hanging from the ceiling! The entire house was heated, and to top it off there were indoor bathrooms. I had hit the jackpot!

Mrs. Yokum was incredibly kind when she spoke to me, and she always looked directly into my eyes. I found it curious when she said she was happy to meet me, as I had never heard those words before. She also said she was glad Beverly had found a nice friend like me. I listened to her words, yet I was a little skeptical about why she thought it was all right that her beautifully dressed daughter had become friends with a little girl wearing a boy's hand-me-down shirt and jeans. In spite of my confusion, I liked her a lot. She always had delicious treats and joyous conversation ready for me when I visited, and the kitchen always carried the aroma of freshly-baked cookies. She doted on Beverly in a manner that was nothing less than magical. It was better than anything on "Donna Reed." It was real.

That first visit, Beverly took me upstairs to her room, which was decorated with fanciful nursery rhyme pictures on the walls and frilly curtains on the windows. She had lots of dolls and toys and a beautiful bed with colorful pink and blue blankets and pillows. Her doll collection was especially intriguing to me, for the dolls were of different sizes and shapes with a variety of eye colors and skin tones. The dolls' hair could actually be combed, and their heads, arms, and legs were movable. Beverly had a little oven in which you could bake real cookies, and she had a wonderful miniature playhouse. I truly believed I had landed on the set of one of those make-believe television programs.

I spent as much time at Beverly's house as I dared. I knew that if I got back to school after the final lunch bell, the superintendent might call my parents to tell them where I had been. Worse, if I missed the bus ride home at the end of the day because I had stopped at Beverly's house, my mother would be called to pick me up, and there would be horrible consequences. Luck was on my side as neither of those events ever happened. I told my mother that Beverly and I were friends, but I never let her know that I went to her house.

In fact, going to Beverly's house was very important to me. It gave me my first glimpse into a home where the parents clearly loved each other and their children and where, whatever challenges the parents may have faced, they were caring, warm, generous, and playful. Over 50 years have gone by since the first time Beverly and I ran that three-legged race together. Since then, we have been a part of each other's weddings, shared each other's excitement over the births of our children, and gone on to live our lives. It has been a long time since we had a physical tie binding our legs together. It was long ago replaced with an unbreakable bond that connects our hearts. Even today, though, we are still running our race together.

❧ Juanita ❧

There were a group of buildings on the farm known as the "Mexican shacks." They were located at the entrance to our property, immediately to the left of the road that led into the farm, about a quarter of a mile from our house. As young children, we were forbidden to go near the shacks and we were told to avoid that area when we walked to the end of the road where the school bus picked us up. The reason my parents gave us for not associating with the Mexicans was that they were not like us, they were dirty and they spoke a different language.

As I mentioned before, I chose to withhold from my mother the fact that I was going to Beverly's house. By the time I was six, I liked making my own choices, even if some of them had to be kept secret. I began to feel more empowered with each decision I made, whether it was picking out my clothes or picking out my friends. Therefore, when I was told I was not allowed to go near the foreign visitors, I could come up with no good reason for that directive to apply to me. Instead, I planned to satisfy my curiosity and go over to the Mexican shacks as soon as I could.

We raised sugar beets on our farm, which entailed a great deal of manual labor. The United States Department of Agriculture would bring Hispanic migrant workers up from Texas to hoe, thin, and weed these crops. Farmers, including sharecroppers like my father and my uncle Bernard, would enter into contracts to employ these laborers and would also agree to provide living arrangements for them and their families. The families would live on our farm during the four-to-six-week hoeing season, and then move on to another farming area.

The migrant housing on our farm was a slum. At any one time, there were about 30 people living in six one-bedroom dwellings. The houses were poorly constructed wooden shacks with tar roofs and they were seldom painted or repaired. Each house had one bed for the parents and mattresses on the floor for the children. Most of the houses did not have running water, and everyone shared the communal outhouse. The area in each shack the occupants used as the kitchen contained a portable two-burner range and a small refrigerator. The aroma of heavily spiced food permeated the houses and floated into the yard when a front door was left open. A communal washing machine was located in a tin shed outside one of the houses. The dogs that traveled with the migrant workers ran wild in the yard.

Every member of the family went into the fields to work under the hot prairie sun. The children who could manage a hoe would work alongside their parents. The younger children would be tended to by an older child. The family of the supervisor Celso Noriega was the exception to this rule. Celso's wife, Angelina, and his daughter, Juanita, did not have to go out into the fields. They would stay home and do their cooking and cleaning. Many of the migrant families worked for only one summer on our farm, but because the federal government assigned Celso as the migrant labor supervisor on our farm, he and his family returned each summer for several years.

On one of my great adventures, I wandered down to the shacks and walked by Celso's house. The front door was open, and I glanced inside and saw a little girl about my age of six standing beside a woman. The little girl saw me and came to the doorway, staring directly at me. She was a little taller than me, and she had skin the color of milk chocolate and long black hair. Her eyes were even a darker shade of brown than mine. I thought she was as beautiful as Beverly. I stopped, and we eyed each other for a minute. Her mother looked at me tentatively; I believe she knew I was not supposed to be there. I asked the little girl for her name, thinking that she might not understand me, since I was told that the migrant families understood only Spanish. She looked at her mother, who nodded back at her, and then she said "My name is Juanita." I smiled at her, not quite sure what to do next. I ran off, thinking that was a good start.

The next day, I went back and walked directly up to Juanita's house. She was outside with her mother, where they had just dug a relatively large hole in the ground in front of their house. I watched silently as they filled the hole with charcoal. Then they put what appeared to be unhusked corn on top of the coals. I later found out this was the method they used to cook tamales.

When they had finished lighting the coals and covering the hole, I asked Juanita if she wanted to play. She turned to say something in Spanish to her mother, who responded rapidly, and Juanita turned back to me. She said she was allowed to play, but we had to stay in her yard.

I was thrilled. I had found a playmate, and I just knew she was a kindred spirit. Juanita could relate to having a hard life. She traveled from state to state with her parents, living in squalor and missing out on education and childhood play. I loved school, so I knew that not being able to go was unjust and unfair, and I told her so. After leaving the sugar beet fields of North Dakota and Minnesota, the migrant workers would travel back to Texas, harvesting vegetable fields along the way as they made their trip south. Juanita told me that she was able to attend school the months they were back home in Texas, and that is where she had learned English.

Juanita and I would play together whenever we could. We would run races in the field and play with the dolls and toys she had brought with her from Texas. Her dolls were made out of straw and canvas, and their dresses were sewn from the same material from which her mother made Juanita's clothes. The dolls were nothing like Beverly's store-bought dolls with their beautiful porcelain heads and silken clothing, but they were beautiful in their own way and I was grateful that Juanita shared them with me. One of our favorite games was hide-and-seek, and we were allowed to play it as long as we did not leave the compound. Angelina was always watching to make sure we were within eyesight. If some of the other children did not have to work in the field, we would all run races or get involved in a group sport. Sometimes Juanita had to help her mother with chores, and I would be asked to come back later. Sometimes I would wait for her on the step of their house until she was available.

I was not invited to go into Juanita's house very often. I believe that Angelina did not want to have to explain to my parents why I was in their home. The house had one door and a window on each wall. It was the largest of the migrant workers' houses, the only one with two bedrooms, a full stove, a refrigerator, and linoleum on the floors. Although it was old and run down, Angelina kept it spotless.

Sometimes when I visited Juanita, her mother would be making tamales in the outdoor pit. These became a special treat for me. Immediately after the tamales were taken out of the ground, Angelina would unwrap one and remove the husk for me. The moist corn meal surrounding the spicy meat filling would melt in my mouth as I savored these new flavors.

Celso and Angelina had adopted Juanita, and they were extremely protective of her. Juanita explained to me what adoption meant, as I did not understand the concept. She said her parents told her she was special because they had picked her out of several children. After I found out this information, I was very careful not to put her in a situation that could potentially harm her or hurt the parents who adored her. Therefore, I did not take Juanita on any of my journeys to the junkyard or the railroad tracks.

When I first met Juanita, I hid from my parents the fact that I was playing with one of the Mexican children. During the second summer, I became more brazen, and Juanita and I would play together in the pasture or field, under Angelina's watchful eye, and where my father and mother could see us. And ultimately, when Angelina became comfortable letting her daughter leave the yard with me, and she gave us permission, I would march up the dusty dirt road that led to our house, hand in hand with Juanita. No one in my family tried to take my playmate away from me. I was getting older, and the look of determination on my face was beginning to harden.

And so, when my father announced at the beginning of each summer that the "Mexicans had arrived," my family would watch me race to Juanita's house to greet her. And at the end of each summer, she would leave, and our annual adventure would end. That was always a sad day for me. Then one summer, when I was twelve, things changed forever. I ran to greet Juanita at her house, but although Celso and Angelina were there, Juanita was not. In broken English, her parents told me that she had stayed in Texas to finish her education, and she had no plans to return. I was heartbroken. When she sent me a high school graduation picture several years later, I was thrilled. Juanita had turned into a lovely young woman, and those dark brown eyes were still her predominant feature. The hairdo in her picture was identical to the hairdo I wore in my graduation picture. We both had dark, shoulder-length straight hair with the ends flipped up in a tight curl. I found it interesting that a white teenage girl in North Dakota and a Mexican teenage girl in Texas, who had not seen each other for six years, would choose the same hair style at the same time.

Although I could not articulate it as a child, I recognized that even in the rural areas of North Dakota where I lived, a class system was in place. The land barons were in a higher class than the small farm owners. The small farmers who owned their land were held in higher regard than the sharecroppers. And the sharecroppers were elevated above the Mexicans. I discovered early on that human beings seem to have a need to be better than someone else.

But the most important lesson I learned from the migrant workers related to family. Beverly had taught me that the love between parents and a child was wondrous, and that it is possible for a child to feel safe and cherished. I learned the same thing from Juanita, yet she also made me realize that this had nothing to do with the economic circumstances of the family, the color of your skin, the language you spoke, or how long you stayed in one place. To Juanita's family, love was as natural as breathing. I decided Juanita was a very lucky girl, for despite the difficulties of being part of a migrant family, she had what I so desperately wanted.

❧ SCHOOL ❦

I loved elementary school and junior high. School was the one area of my life where there was visible proof that I could excel. Teachers and friends acknowledged me for my academic success. I looked forward to getting my report card each six-week grading period, for it was always full of A's and "satisfactory" check marks. My parents expected that we children would perform well in school, so we did not anticipate (nor did we receive) any praise. In spite of this lack of acknowledgement, I felt deep personal satisfaction at my accomplishments. I still have all of my "Elementary Report Cards," including the original manila envelopes that held them.

The children that lived in town and those of us who were bused in from the outlying farms got our entire education at

Mapleton Elementary and High School. It was a red brick building in the center of town and had approximately 150 students from kindergarten through high school. The elementary classrooms and the administrative offices were on the first floor, the high school classes took place on the upper level. The janitor buffed and polished the tile floors to a high sheen each night. The desks and chairs in the classrooms were made of solid oak and varnished a dark chocolate brown. The desktops lifted up so books and supplies could be stored underneath, and each desktop had a groove in it to rest pencils and an ink well holder (out of style even before I started school). The desks displayed carvings and graffiti, the historical markings left by prior students. Palmer Penmanship Posters, displaying the correct style of writing (at least according to Mr. Palmer) were displayed on the first and second grade classroom walls.

The outdoor playground had two sets of swings, a slide, a teeter-totter, and a merry-go-round. There was a large grassy space for racing and playing games like tag and tug of war. Recess was obligatory, even during the cold winter days, although when the weather was frigid the time outside would be shortened. Starting in the first grade, girls were required to wear dresses every day, a welcome change from the hand-me-downs I wore through kindergarten. My mother obtained some used jumpers and skirts for me, and during the winter months I also brought along pants. When the recess bell rang, we rushed into the cloak room and put on our pants under our dresses and over the long brown or white stockings we were already wearing for warmth. I liked wearing the long pants under my skirts, as they partially hid my brother's old brown shoes that I had to wear through the second grade. In the winter, when we were outside, we ran around a lot more and a lot faster to try to keep warm.

The school was run by Mr. Johnson, the superintendent, whose office was on the first floor near the elementary classrooms. Mr. Johnson wore his hair in a crew cut, so he reminded me of one of the tough army sergeants I saw on television. He did not smile a lot, nor did he seem to enjoy children all that much. School policy allowed any teacher to send a pupil to his office for even the most minor infraction.

Once, in the sixth grade, I had to go to Mr. Johnson's office for running in the lunchroom. He made the experience as unpleasant as possible for me, reminding me about the proper way to behave in school and how to show respect for the teachers. At the end of his lecture, he played his trump card by telling me he would make sure to call my parents if it ever happened again. I sat in silence the entire time, occasionally glancing down at the polished floor. When he finished, I made my obligatory apology before I was dismissed. This was the first time I was sent to Mr. Johnson's office, but definitely not the last time. During my high school years, I would become one of his frequent visitors.

Mrs. Claus, the seventh and eighth grade teacher, would curl up her lips in a closed-mouth grin as she dug the high heel of her shoe into any foot she caught sprawling out into the aisle. Keeping your hands and feet in the "right spot" was very important to her. Mrs. Claus was also famous for rapping the knuckles of disruptive children with her ruler. She demanded order in her classroom, and we spoke only when she gave us permission. During class, hands and arms rested on the desk, pencils were placed in the groove, and the desktop was cleared of any school items not currently being used.

We were to remain silent while Mrs. Claus administered her punishments to a fellow classmate. My relief was mixed with sadness when it was not me having to endure the humiliating punishment. My body would tense up, and often I employed my well-developed skill of not breathing. If the student cried out in pain, I would pretend I did not hear it. Everyone in the room practiced this self-imposed deafness.

One of the boys in my class, Randy, had learning disabilities, and reading was a particular struggle for him. Once a week,

Mrs. Claus selected a student to stand in front of the group to read aloud from a library book. Everyone, including Mrs. Claus, knew that when she picked Randy to read, it would be miserable for him and uncomfortable for everyone in the room. Randy would always urinate in his pants because of his nervous distress over standing in front of the group. I would watch in horror as the wet spot around his zipper would start to expand.

While any child was reading, the rest of us were to remain silent. I followed this order, even when Randy read, but I would surreptitiously move my eyes to catch the reaction of the other children. Some of the girls closed their eyes against Randy's torture. Some blinked back tears. Most of the boys sat stunned with embarrassment. Some looked down at their desktops and traced the carvings with their fingers. Sometimes, a nervous giggle escaped from someone who could no longer contain his or her emotions. This usually resulted in a wooden-ruler knuckle-rapping.

When Randy faltered or stumbled on a word, Mrs. Claus would shout the correct pronunciation from the back of the room. On Randy's day, the entire hour of the reading class was devoted to this process. At the end of the selection Mrs. Claus had told him to read, Randy would speed back to his desk with his head down, and slink into his chair. Mrs. Claus said nothing, and the students said nothing. I first learned about not talking and not telling at my house, and these same lessons were reinforced at school.

I never mentioned any of these events to my parents, for they had elevated all teachers to a god-like status. In my household, the teacher was always right, in both speech and action.

A part of me wishes that Mrs. Claus was still alive to read this book, for perhaps she would agree that she made at least one error in judgment back then. In the seventh grade, she gave me a "C" in writing. Using one of her sharpest tones, she explained "You got that grade because you never listen to me in class." Her assessment was that by asking for clarification on an assignment, I must not have been listening in the first place, or I would not have needed the additional instructions.

Mrs. Claus was wrong. I was listening to everything.

❧ MAPLETON ❧

Mapleton, where we went to school, was a six-mile drive from our farm on a series of gravel and dirt roads. Mailboxes for the farms in our area were clustered together at one place for the convenience of the postman. Our box was on a gravel road exactly a mile from the farm, which meant that six days a week one of us kids would make the two-mile walk to pick up the mail. Fortunately, the school bus stopped right in front of the entrance to our farm, so we did not also have to make a long trek back and forth to catch the bus.

In 1950, Mapleton boasted a population of 169. There was a general store that also housed the post office, a hardware store, a restaurant with an adjacent bar (my father's nightly hangout), the Presbyterian Church, and a town hall. The cooperative grain elevator, where the farmers would sell and store their harvested crops until they were shipped by rail to the grain mills, was central to the business life of the town. The Northern Pacific Railroad passed directly through the heart of Mapleton, connecting it to Fargo and the other larger cities of the Midwest. Most of the farm families would do their main grocery and farm supply shopping in Castleton and Fargo. For those of us living in the rural areas, the Mapleton stores were a convenience when we did not want to make a longer trip.

I expect that life in the small town of Mapleton would seem very boring by today's standards, but back then it was lively and exciting to me. Beverly's mom and dad were very well liked in Mapleton, and everybody knew them and their children. In first grade, my parents asked if I had made any friends. I told them about Beverly, but I never told them about going to her house. As we became closer, Beverly and I spent more and more time with each other. We would have grand times together as we explored the town, and we were greeted by everyone. Beverly would take me to Derrig's Grocery Store, and we would buy the penny candy they had displayed in bins at the front counter. Her mom always supplied us with the necessary pennies. I can still remember biting the ends off of miniature wax soda bottles and sucking out some sugary fluid. I am not sure today that I want to know what that really was!

Our school was kept immaculately clean, and its playground was well maintained. There were actually white picket fences around the beautifully-manicured yards of Mapleton's residents. Everything was in order in Mayberry, USA. Well, almost everything.

At times, Beverly and I would make a visit to the general store or the post office, and I would stop and listen to adults talking about one of the families in town. When they noticed I was paying attention, their voices would lower to whispers, yet I still could hear the names Paulson, Gustafson, Carroll, and Watson.

The voices whispered the most frequently about the Adamson family. The Adamson house was filled with four boys, each of whom, to one degree or another, had a reputation of being a town bad boy or bully. I had never heard my parents speak about that family, so I was interested in what the town people had to say.

David, the youngest of the Adamson boys, was in my grade. I must admit that he did give everyone fodder for their gossip. He was always getting in trouble, spending time in the superintendent's office and being kicked out of school. My recollection is that he was sent off to a juvenile detention center for a while. He had been branded a delinquent, and that was the way he was treated by the town and by the teachers.

I liked David. He had blond hair, a sweet face, and a devilish grin. Most of the other children were afraid of him, yet I was not. I think there was a secret kinship between us, although we made an odd pair. I was withdrawn and shy and always acted like a "good girl" at school; David was volatile. I do not know if I liked him because of this attribute or in spite of it. I sensed he had honed his survival skills through his speed, agility, and daredevil ways, and I admired him for it.

I remember David coming to school on many occasions with a variety of bruises and fractures. I do not think any of us children—even me—thought much about it, since we all knew that he and his brothers engaged in physical fights with one another. At least that was the explanation David gave us for his injuries.

I recall that once, during a school year, David was absent for a few days. Although this was not unusual, this time when he returned both of his hands were completely wrapped in gauze, making it seem like he was wearing boxing gloves. He told us all a story of bravery and bravado. He had tried to climb over a wall with lines of barbed wire across the top, and he had slashed open his hands holding onto the wire as he jumped over.

David had lied about the barbed wire. In truth, he had displeased his father and as punishment he had been taken down to the basement, where his hands were held over the open flames of the wood-burning stove and seared like burned steaks. I learned about this long after it happened, when I got my first job and was living in Minneapolis and roomed for a short time with a girl from Mapleton. Her family lived near David's, and she told me about this and about many other abusive punishments that had taken place in that basement.

The residents of Mapleton knew what was going on in the Adamson household in the 1950s, at the time it was happening. With only 169 people, the town was very small, and everybody made it their business to know your business. I am dumbfounded by the lack of community involvement in helping the Adamson children. Perhaps the adults were afraid of repercussions from the abusive father. Perhaps nobody really knew what to do, so they did nothing. And, sad as it may be, perhaps the existence of the Adamsons as scapegoats eased the pain and guilt others felt about their own behavior with their children. The Adamson family dynamic may have served a valuable purpose for the town.

Whatever the reason, no neighbors, friends, teachers, or school administrators came forward to help any of the children in Mapleton. And no one came forward to help the children on the farms either.

❧ Not-So-Sweet Sixteen ❧

I excelled academically throughout grade school and junior high. As a freshman, I won a spot on the varsity cheerleading squad alongside Beverly, the bond we had formed in kindergarten still intact. She and I developed some "cool" gymnastic moves that garnered us first place in the state cheerleading contest. I was at the top of my class, involved in various school activities, and I enjoyed hanging around with my friends. I acted much like the other teenagers around me, and outwardly I gave the appearance of being happy and of loving high school. Inside there was a storm brewing.

At the end of my sophomore year, I got into a shouting match with my mother, and it ended in physical violence. We were in the kitchen when an argument escalated into angry threats on both of our parts, and she went out to the porch to get the oak laundry stick. When she returned, something flared up inside of me—the rage from years of abuse—and this was the day it would come out. I grabbed the stick from her, and with a strength that came from that rage, I snapped the inch-thick oak rod in half. Then I grabbed my mother on either side of her waist, lifted her up, and threw her against the washing machine. She groaned in pain and sank to the floor. I could literally smell her fear, and I could taste my rage. I screamed at her, "If you ever fucking touch me again, I will kill you!"

I stormed out of the house, jumped in the family truck, and took off for town.

I returned to the house that evening. My mother said nothing to me, and I said nothing to her. We never fought or argued again. In fact, we spoke very little after that event. I do not know if my mother spoke to my father about our fight, but if she did, he never talked about it to me.

That summer I took a job with Barbara and her family, farmers in a neighboring town, serving as the live-in maid, nanny, and cook. I had started babysitting at Barbara's house when I was fourteen, mostly on weekends. She and her husband had three children, two boys and a girl, all under the age of five. I was excited about being able to earn some money for myself, and I also wanted to escape from the antagonist relationship with my mother and the possibility of another argument that would become physical. I told my mother and father what I was going to do, not asking for their permission. They just nodded their heads and expressed neither approval nor disapproval.

Before starting, I told Barbara that I did not know how to cook, and I proved it when I started a grease fire in their kitchen. They took me off that duty. The living arrangement with them provided me with the distance I needed from my mother to avoid another explosive encounter. After the summer, I moved back home but continued working part-time for Barbara. My father bought me an old Cavalier that I used to drive from the house to my job and also to school and various activities. The car was old, leaked oil, and needed a paint job, but it ran and it got me where I wanted and needed to be. During this period of my life, my mother and I continued to have very little interaction. We ignored each other when we were in the house at the same time.

As I began my junior year, I soon discovered that the Anger Genie who was released from her bottle at the start of that summer was still on a rampage. She appeared when I encountered an authority figure at school, and she was not going to be corked up again. I did not know how to deal with what had been unleashed. I took my anger out by rebelling against the teachers and the administration, especially Mr. Johnson, whom I defied every chance I got. On several occasions, my quips, comments, and comebacks landed me in his office for a lecture on respecting adults. He never asked me if I thought that adults should respect children, and I did not offer my opinion.

Mr. Johnson labeled me a juvenile delinquent, and by the standards of the day, he was right. I disrupted classrooms, had fights with other students, and was an all-around screw-up. He did nothing to inquire about the cause of the change in my behavior, and, looking back, I believe he lacked the training and skills even to know that he should do so.

I spent a lot of time in the library, which served double duty as the detention center for anyone kicked out of class. If Mr. Johnson felt my actions were more egregious than usual, he would kick me out of school for the day. I would use this "opportunity" to drive into Casselton or Fargo, returning to the schoolyard in time to pick up my sister, who needed a ride home.

As much trouble as I caused in school, the only time Mr. Johnson ever called my parents about my behavior was when I set my Cavalier on fire in the school parking lot. Smoking was forbidden on the school grounds—if you got caught, you would immediately be suspended. One spring day, two of my male classmates and I decided we would drive into town during the lunch break to have a cigarette. We drove around Mapleton, smoking and feeling we had really "stuck it to the man!" We came back just before the bell rang, put our cigarettes out, and rushed into the school.

Midway through the afternoon, an announcement was made over the loud speaker that I was to proceed directly to Mr. Johnson's office. I walked to his office—a familiar location for me by then—wondering what trouble I was in this time. He told me that the fire department had been called because the custodian had noticed that the back seat of my car was on fire and it needed to be ripped out so the entire car would not go up in flames. He said someone had left a smoldering cigarette in the backseat ashtray, and it had fallen out onto the upholstery. He wanted to know if I had been smoking in my car, a question he already knew the answer to. What he really wanted to know was if I had any accomplices. By this time I could lie with the best of them, and I adamantly professed my sole responsibility for the act. He kept pushing me, but I never ratted on my classmates. I saved my friends from getting into trouble, and I got suspended for three days.

My father arrived at the school to pick me up and have the car towed away to the repair shop. All he said as we otherwise drove home in silence, was that I was going to have to pay for the repairs. He was not about to rage like his father—he just let the anger simmer inside of himself. I viewed the school expulsion as a nuisance, not a deterrent to my bad behavior. This would have been a great opportunity for my father to impose repercussions for my actions and to establish boundaries for me. I know that if he would have done just that, it would have had a positive impact on me, for that is what I so desperately needed in my life. I was crying out for boundaries, not like the inappropriate ones that came from my mother's personal rage, but the type that would come from an adult who saw a teenager needing to learn to take responsibility for her own actions. My father never taught me to do this, and I thought that I could get away with almost anything.

During my junior year, I started hanging around with Donna. Donna was one of "those" girls. I liked her, or at least was very curious about her, since her behavior was unpredictable, and she was usually in trouble because of it. We had an unspoken bond of sorts, for I understood why she acted as she did. When I would visit her house, I would observe how her father and brothers stared at her fully developed body, and I would hear the titillating words they used with her. I knew intuitively that Donna was involved in a struggle in her house. Like me, she made it her business to be away from her home as much as she could. So the two of us would go into Fargo every Saturday night to drink, cruise up and down the midway, and generally carouse around town. Most of the time, I would drive my Cavalier (which my father fixed for me after the fire) unless Donna could talk her parents into letting her use one of their cars.

One night, the Fargo Police stopped Donna and me and demanded that we get out of the car. I fully expected that I was going to get busted for drunk driving, so I was surprised when they announced we were going to be taken to the station for solicitation for prostitution. Apparently, Donna had been willing to do things that I had not yet thought about! The events that happened after that are fuzzy, mostly due to the amount of beer I had consumed during the course of the evening. I do remember Donna's mom coming to get us out of jail. In those days, when juveniles got in trouble in rural areas, even in Fargo, the parents were called to collect their offspring. The police lectured the kids about "never seeing them back here again" and then turned them over to the parents for punishment. I stayed at Donna's house that night, and the next day she drove me back to Fargo to pick up my car. When I returned home, nobody in my house, parents or siblings, asked where I was during my two days with Donna. I also never went carousing with her again. I still liked Donna, but after this episode, I decided her lifestyle was a bit too dangerous even for my tastes.

Before I stopped hanging out with Donna, I met a young man named Greg during one of our escapades. He was tall, drop-dead gorgeous, had black wavy hair, and was deliciously dangerous. The day I met him, he had been released from the county jail and was out on parole for a crime I did not ask about. What a perfect combo we made! I thought it would be a great idea to invite him to one of the school dances with me, where I could show my small-town friends what I had found in the big city of Fargo. Mr. Johnson's jaw dropped to the floor as Greg and I walked into the school auditorium together. By then I had developed a totally antagonistic relationship with our superintendent, and he was always gunning for me. He came up to Greg and asked him if he had permission to leave the city of Fargo. Greg's beautiful face paled as he shook his head "no." Mr. Johnson ordered him to leave the school immediately, and told me I should do the same. I could feel the blood drain from my face when Mr. Johnson told me that he also served as a part-time parole officer in Fargo, and he knew Greg from the court system. Oh my God, I was so screwed!

I paid dearly for my display of in-your-face attitude, as Mr. Johnson meted out the most devastating punishment he could have devised. He refused to let me serve on the basketball cheerleading squad. I was furious with him at the time, and I was embarrassed and ashamed to go from being a state champion cheerleader to being kicked off the squad. I had lost the opportunity to do something that I was very good at, that I was proud of, and that I loved.

By the middle of my junior year, something deep inside of me was telling me that I was in trouble and headed down a road to nowhere. I could not get over the humiliation of being barred from cheerleading, and I felt the need to redeem myself, mostly in my own eyes. I told myself my senior year was going to be different, and that I was going to get back on track and be a cheerleader again. With the benefit of hindsight, I owe Mr. Johnson a debt of gratitude, despite his other shortcomings, for his punishment was the reason I became more respectful to the teachers, if only to get back on the cheerleading squad.

Focusing on good, hard physical work often helped me get my head on straight. The summer between my junior and senior years, I took a job hoeing sugar beets. I talked Beverly into doing this with me, as I did not want to be the only girl going out into the fields. She agreed to accompany me, only because I told her we would make a fortune. We were picked up in Mapleton in the dark morning hours, and loaded into the wooden bed of a rickety truck. There were twenty migrant Mexican workers, Beverly, and me. The other workers looked at us like we were aliens, so we kept to ourselves. We stood up in the flat truck bed, hanging onto its wooden sides for dear life as we were jostled the entire ten-mile trip into the fields.

By the time we reached our destination, the sun was up, and we were given hoeing and thinning instructions and put to work. It was June and well over 100 degrees in the fields. For eight hours a day, we walked up and down mile-long rows of recently sprouted plants. Using wooden-handled hoes, we removed the weeds and thinned out the young sugar beet plants. The supervisor would stand at the beginning and end of each row with a big jug of water for all of us to drink from, a sort of carrot and stick incentive. We got to stop for a half-hour lunch break, and two fifteen-minute water breaks. Beverly and I hoed side by side, keeping each other company in the sweltering heat. In spite of the heavy work gloves we wore, the motion of pushing and pulling the hoe through the dirt caused huge blisters to form on our hands. Our backs ached from constantly bending over during the one-mile march up and down the field.

At the end of the day, we were covered with black dirt and dust, which was by now glued to our sweaty bodies. We returned back to Mapleton exhausted, aching, and filthy. I will never forget the look on Beverly's mom face when she saw her daughter get off the truck, as she was now indistinguishable from the migrant workers. And I will definitely remember Beverly's expression when she received her cash payment of one dollar for each row she had hoed. I believe we each made eight dollars that day.

Beverly never went back into the sugar beet fields with me. I finished up my self-imposed two weeks of corporal punishment, earned about $300, and then returned to my live-in summer babysitting job for Barbara. Changing diapers was a welcome relief.

I started my senior year in a more humble state of mind, for I wanted to get back on the cheerleading squad (which I did!). I felt more in charge of my life and my future than I ever had. I realized that I could earn my own money, and I settled back into my academic studies and other activities with a renewed confidence. My family and I stayed out of each other's way. My mother and I just plain avoided each other. My father and I were becoming strangers, as I was home very little. When I was not at school or involved in an afterschool activity, I was babysitting or hanging out with my friends. My brother was in college, and we had little contact. I had developed a sharp edge to my personality by this time and it said to my family, "Stay away," and they did.

My grandmother Blanche had left her parents' house at sixteen to marry in an attempt to legitimize her child born of abuse. My aunt Ruby Mae had fled my grandfather's house on her sixteenth birthday to escape his abusive treatment of her. During the summer I turned sixteen, I worked full-time for Barbara and lived at her house, since this helped me to escape the dysfunction in my family. Our ancestral history seemed destined to keep repeating itself.

❧ BARBARA'S HOUSE ❦

Barbara was unlike any of the other farm wives I knew. Most of their lives revolved around child rearing, cooking, and housekeeping. Barbara preferred to hire me for those chores so she could pursue her political activities. She was the president of the League of Women Voters and a staunch supporter of the Equal Rights Amendment. She spoke at public events, wrote articles for the Fargo newspaper, and was in the process of getting her law degree. She educated me about the rights of women and became a great role model for my future feminist activities.

I did not speak to Barbara in any great detail about my child-hood. The reason I gave her for wanting to stay with her family was to earn money, which was partially true. When she made the statement that it seemed like my mother and I did not get along, I told her it was just part of my teenage rebellion. I had never talked to anybody about my childhood, and by this time the practice of silence was so ingrained, it was a part of my nature. Barbara had become a mother figure to me, I was in a comfortable situation living in her house, and I didn't want anything to possibly destroy it.

I was an angry teenager with emotions I did not understand and no skills to control them. The physical altercation with my mother was evidence of the rage that was teeming beneath the surface, waiting for another chance for me to express it. One day Barbara's husband gave me that opportunity, after his wife left for Fargo to buy groceries. He came into the kitchen, waving a package of condoms in front of me, telling me we were going to go up to the bedroom. I took a butcher knife out of the drawer, pointed it at him, and said, "And afterwards I will cut off your balls tonight while you are sleeping." My explosion turned out to be an effective deterrent, as he never suggested sex to me again for the dura-tion of my stay. I never spoke to anyone about this, for the practice of silence again prevailed.

At the time, I did not think about why I had reacted so violently to his behavior. It would be years later before I came to a full understanding. As I mentioned, I never spoke to anyone about this event. Except for Barbara, I could not think of anyone who would have cared. And if I told her, I knew I would have been sent back home, and I desperately wanted to stay with her. So I stayed in the house for the rest of that summer, and continued as Barbara's helper—my eyes always alert—until I graduated high school.

Barbara had a tremendous influence on my decision to go to college. During my senior year I settled down into a more relaxed less angry state of mind, and I started to date a nice young man who farmed with his father. We became engaged and decided to get married right after I graduated. His plan was to take over his father's farm and for me to become a North Dakota housewife. Barbara thought very little of this idea, and she told me so in no uncertain terms. Employing the debate techniques she developed at the League, she challenged me, in great detail, about why I would want to waste my intellect and talent by determining my future before I had a chance to explore my options. She told me that a life on the farm would be there for me, if I still wanted it, after I graduated from college. She also suggested that marriage was not always everything it was reputed to be, knowledge I had already acquired.

Barbara and I had several discussions and debates about my future. Finally it clicked for me that college would be the best option to create a better life for myself and the type of future I wanted. I made this announcement to my future husband, who immediately decided that my new plans were not going to work with his plans. Our engagement soon ended. I sobbed as I told this to Barbara. She was politely sympathetic, yet I am pretty sure I saw a look of relief on her face.

There was one huge hurdle in the way of my college plans: I did not have the money to go to school. When I told this to Barbara, she said if I wanted it badly enough I could make it happen. Once challenged, I established a plan to earn enough money for the first year's tuition. I figured I would deal with the issue of room and board when I got to school. Tuition was $1,100 at the state university, and that was a fortune to me. The thought of hoeing sugar beets was not appealing, so I came up with something less backbreaking. I worked as a waitress in Fargo on weekends and babysat whenever I could during the week. During the summer I continued to work as live-in help. I saved every dollar I earned, which was enough money for my tuition.

Saying goodbye to Barbara the day before I left for college was extremely difficult. She had fulfilled a strong parental role in my life, and now she was gently pushing me out of the nest. She said, "Marion, I'm so proud of you, and I know you'll accomplish great things in your life." Then she handed me a shopping bag from a department store in Fargo. In it were three skirts and three blouses, with a note that said, "So you can feel like a real college student." I have purchased lots of nice clothing since that time, yet none of it has meant as much to me as the wardrobe I received that day.

Barbara wrote notes to me at college, always wanting to know how I was doing. I remember how wonderful it felt to write back to her, sending along a copy of my first perfect 4.0 grade report. She wrote back in her flowing, large handwriting, "I knew you could do it."

❧ DADDY'S NOT-SO-LITTLE GIRL ❧

By the time I finished high school, my father and I were not really speaking. Actually, from the time I was fifteen and started driving, my father and I had less and less interaction, not that we had that much when I was a little child. I had become fiercely independent, especially after I learned how to earn my own money, and I spent little time around the house. Having a car added to my freedom, and I pretty much came and went as I pleased during my high school years.

As always, my father spent almost all of his free time in Mapleton, drinking at the bar and playing cards. On occasion we would get a telephone call from the bar owner, letting us know that my father was "in no shape" to be driving home. In those days, the tolerance for people getting drunk and driving was extremely high, so if one of the bartenders called us, my father's consumption was nearing alcohol poisoning or a complete blackout.

If my brother or I were home when the call came in, my

mother dispatched one of us to go into town and pick up Dad and bring him home. I do not recall my mother making any of these trips herself. I fetched him on several occasions, and he was never happy when I would appear. He was mad that someone had called us; according to him he was "just fine" and could drive himself home. The bar owner would chide him that he needed to go home with me, and after some coaxing, he would usually give in and get in the car. If he refused to come along, I did not argue with him, I just left him at the bar to get a ride with one of his buddies. After making a few of these trips, I really did not care if he got home or not. Later in life, I came to understand what devastating events such drunkenness could lead to. At the time I did not comprehend that it could end in killing not only yourself, but other people as well. I was just too angry at my father to even think about that.

One night, I was sent to pick him up. I was not terribly happy about it, as I had a lot of homework to do. When I got into town, I found him swaying on one of the bar stools, rubbing the leg of one of my female schoolmates who was waiting there for her father. She sat stiffly, not knowing what to do, with a look of embarrassment and humiliation on her face. I glared at him, repulsed, and told him to "get his own fucking ride home," and I left him to fend for himself. He was at our breakfast table the next morning. Either he had driven himself home, or he had gotten a ride. I did not care which, and nobody talked about it. No one in the family ever discussed picking up Dad in town or any of his behavior related to drinking. We all pretended that nothing had happened, for in those days nothing had happened; it was just "normal." I ran into that schoolmate in the hall at school the next day, and we just passed each other and kept walking. Nothing was said between us, for in those days nothing was supposed to be said.

Although I did not spend time dwelling on it, my respect for my father diminished during this period. As a little girl,

I had held onto the idea that he was my white knight. And even though he had never arrived to save me, my sense of survival somehow depended on my believing that he would. Those dreams dwindled and died when, as a teenager, I was the one who started saving him.

✑ Free at Last ✑

My grandfather Frank left Germany at seventeen to travel to America for greater opportunities. My grandfather Oliver traveled across country at twenty to make a new life for himself. I could certainly travel less than a hundred miles for the same freedom.

I was frightened as I began college in a town 80 miles north of the farm, yet my fear was tempered by the excitement of starting a new life. Now I could put everything that happened in the past behind me. There was no reason for me to give another thought to abuse, neglect, abandonment, or isolation. That was my childhood, and it was over. I was a young adult now, and I could carve out the life I wanted.

My mother and father were ambivalent about my going to college. My dad said that it would probably be a waste of time and money, since I would get married after I graduated and never work anyway. I begged him to please pay for the first semester of room and board, and to give me a chance to see what I could do. He reluctantly agreed. I completed the first semester and attained perfect grades. I was also on a school/work program, through which I was employed in the campus cafeteria to earn my spending money. Things were going well. Then, just as I was registering for my second semester, my brother dropped out of college in his senior year of engineering school. My father was furious with him, and his anger spilled over on to me. He said he was not going to waste any more of his money on his kids' education. When he made this announcement I became furious, told him I could "take care of myself," and hung up the phone. I was so accustomed to being abandoned by him that for a while I actually got angry at myself for being stupid enough to think maybe this time my father would be different.

At first I went into panic mode, wondering if I was going to be able to stay in school. Then, acting on the lesson I had learned at Barbara's instigation, I went into action and developed a plan to pay for my room and board. I picked up two more jobs so that I would be able to pay my dormitory costs. In the morning I was a food server in the school cafeteria, after my last class I did clerical work at the office of the Dean of Women, and in the evening I answered the telephone for a sales and marketing company. I also stayed on campus all year and attended summer school. In this way, I was able to complete my degree in three years as a means of avoiding the expense of a fourth year.

I was driven to succeed and also to "show my family" I did not need them. My hard work ended with mixed results. I graduated first in my class, I was exhausted, and I was severely underweight. It was all worth it, though, for I had gotten my education and I was hired by a national accounting firm in Minneapolis, where I was to begin working that summer. There was a wonderful life awaiting me, and I had proved my parents wrong! I showed them that girls do finish school, and I did it on my own.

While in college, occasionally I made visits home for the holidays. I participated in the traditional family meal and visited with relatives. I had long since stopped attending the Catholic Church, so I declined offers to join in the religious ceremonies. My brother enlisted in the Army after dropping out of college, so generally he was not home. My sister lived with my parents, as she was still in high school. We played at being sisters, shopping and visiting friends, but we were never close. I had spent so much time on my own as a child that, when she was growing up, we never really got to know each other. Because my brother had begun to protect her when she was a toddler and to drop his protective attitude toward me, by the time I was five I did not feel needed by either of them and was more comfortable being by myself.

Other than holiday visits, I had little contact with my family during my three years of college. My interactions with my parents during this time were limited and superficial. My mother and father attended my graduation, and they said they were proud of my accomplishments. I was proud too—that I had done it without them.

I thought everything was great. Well, maybe I was a little angry, but I would use my anger as an incentive. Perhaps I drank a bit too much now and then, but what was the harm in that? I had trouble trusting people, but didn't everyone to some extent? I could work through these minor issues. Everyone has problems of one sort or another, I reasoned, so mine were no big deal. I believed nothing could stop me from having a wonderful life and nothing could get in my way. I would discover that something was going to do just that. It was my past, and I would have to deal with it sooner or later.

❧ Not Free, Not Even Close ❧

The physical abuse during my childhood left me feeling like I was unlovable. As a child, with a limited ability to think rationally but needing to gain some type of understanding of my life, I came to believe that since I needed to be punished so harshly, I must be a "bad little girl." I tried to be a good, but the definition of "good" turned out to be a moving target. No matter what I did, nothing was ever good enough. I felt angry, frightened, and vulnerable.

The neglect left me feeling like an orphan, as though I never had a mom or dad. As a sensitive little girl wanting to be heard and seen, I was pressured to dress like a little boy and punished when I resisted. I looked liked a ragamuffin, and I thought I was worthless. I felt ashamed, invisible, and unwanted.

The abandonment I experienced when my father did not protect me, and my brother turned on me, would leave lifelong emotional scars. Since the people in my life did not protect me when I was in danger and left me when I needed them the most, I did not believe anyone could be trusted. I felt disappointed, hurt, and rejected.

The isolation of living on the remote prairie farm, coupled with the limited contact with the outside world during my earliest formative years, provided the perfect breeding ground for the undetected and unreported abuse. Distance was a recurring theme in my childhood. I felt distant from my immediate family, as though I did not belong. The distance forced upon the relatives that lived so close to me on the farm further added to my feeling of isolation. In my eyes, I was totally alone in the world. I felt sad, lonely, and despondent.

I now understand that none of my needs as a child had been met. I never felt safe, respected, cared for, or protected. And I did not feel loved. These needs had been replaced with shame, guilt, fear, and anger. As a child I did not understand the complex situation I was being raised in, and there was no one to speak to about it. As a teenager, thoughts of hatred for my family started to fill my mind, along with the desire for retaliation and revenge. It was at that time that I decided I would never forgive them for what had happened. I would leave home, never look back, be free of my childhood, and everything would be fine.

As a young adult, I still believed this. But it was just wishful thinking. Actually, although I had no conscious awareness of this at the time, I was in a prison of emotional and psychological damage.

❧ FAMILY PHOTO ALBUM ❧

1910 Josephine & Oliver Serum
My maternal Norwegian grandparents, Oliver and Josephine Serum, were married in 1910. True to the cultural stereotype, they were hardworking, silent types.

1920 Blanche, Ruby, Alvin, Bernard
My paternal grandmother, Blanche Witte, with her daughter Ruby and sons Alvin and Bernard in 1920. By the time she was 27, Blanche had six young children and an abusive, alcoholic husband.

1933 Frank Witte family
Frank and Blanche Witte surrounded by their children in 1933. At far left, my father Alvin, who in many ways grew up to emulate his own father—filled with anger.

1950s Farm

*After school and on weekends I would roam the land and abandoned buildings
surrounding the farm. No one ever came looking for me. My siblings and I never
played with our cousins, who lived on the same land, due to some long-simmering
family tensions.*

1948 Frankie & Marion on farm house step
My big brother Frankie keeps me safe on the
porch of our farmhouse in 1948.

**1949 Marion & Frankie in Grand Forks,
North Dakota**
In high spirits, Frankie and I race each other on
a sidewalk in front of a relative's apartment in
Grand Forks, North Dakota, in 1949.

**1951 Frank, Claudia &
Marion on farm house step**
By the age of 3, I was
no longer the subject
of my brother Frankie's
protective impulses, which
he transferred to my younger
sister Claudia.

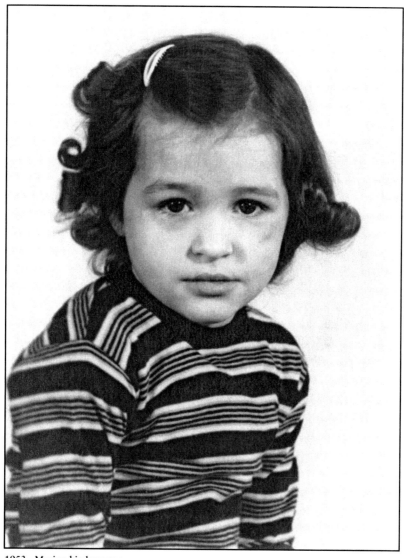

1953 Marion-kindergarten
In my kindergarten class photo I wear a barrette in my hair and a bruise on my cheek. If anyone thought something might have been wrong in the Witte home, no one ever dared to step forward.

1953 Beverly's birthday
Even celebrating my best friend Beverly's birthday, I wear a somber expression. Her home offered my first glimpse of a warm and happy family life.

1955 Witte Children-after church
It was important that we look like the perfect family each Sunday at church. Who would guess the truth?

1966   Juanita graduation (hair flip)
Although her family was poor, Juanita's parents lavished their daughter with love and welcomed me into their home…

1966   Marion graduation (hair flip)
…Our 1966 high school graduation photos capture two teenage girls who share identical tastes in the hairstyle du jour—the "flip."

1971   Marion at Deloitte (all business)
A career as a successful accountant at one of the "Big 8" accounting firms satisfied my drive for perfection and a need to constantly prove myself. My 1971 official company portrait says it all.

1974   Gloria Steinem years
Babushka, tinted aviator glasses and groovy striped pants announce my feminist credentials: I am woman, hear me roar!

1983 Grandma & Grandpa in Chicago
My wonderful in-laws, Angelo and Catherine Scaletta, provided the parental role models I never had. My beautiful daughter Angela, a year old in 1983, taught me about unconditional love.

1985 California Or Bust— Marion, Paul & Angela
With husband Paul and daughter Angela, I stage our annual family Christmas card. The theme, in 1985, was our recent move to California, complete with wacky costumes.

2001 Angela USC Graduation (Angela & Marion)
A proud mother, I celebrate my daughter Angela's graduation from the University of Southern California.

2005 Foundation kick-off
The launch of my Angel Heart Foundation marks the beginning of my work to make sure all children have the right to live lives free of mental and physical cruelty. No wonder I'm smiling.

❧ THE JOURNEY ❧

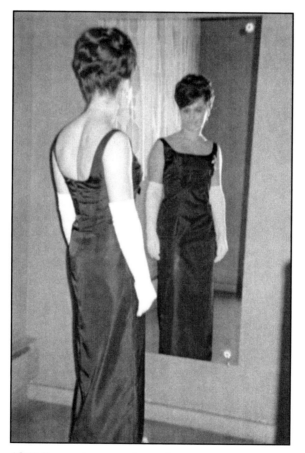

1967 Fraternity party bound
On my way to a fraternity party in 1967, I take a last look and seem to ask: Mirror, mirror, on the wall... who is the girl looking back at me? Who is Marion Witte? Will I ever get to know her?

THE PAST ALWAYS COMES KNOCKING,
AND SOMETIMES IT DOESN'T CALL FIRST.

Marion Witte

❧ PRETENDING ❦

When I graduated from college, I visited my Aunt Bertha in California. I remember my outrage when she boldly asked me, "What happened to you on that farm?" I thought carefully about how I was going to answer. I wondered why she would ask such a question and whether she could possibly know anything about what had occurred in our house. Trying to maintain the facade that we were a "normal" family, I eventually said, "Nothing happened. Everything was fine." I could tell she thought I was lying. Was I losing my talent for pretending?

I visited my Aunt Lorine a few years later and she also tried to crack the armament I had placed around myself. She and Bertha must have been comparing notes, since she asked me a similar question. My mind flashed back to the time when she found me soaked in my own urine, the time she was so compassionate toward me. Even though I was still denying how extreme my mother's actions actually were, I knew how bizarre, or at least upsetting, my being forced to stay in that wet bed must have appeared to my aunt. Still, fifteen years later, rather than answer my Aunt Lorine honestly, I gave her a puzzled look and changed the subject, a talent I had finely tuned.

This technique helped me to obey the rule of silence that I had learned so well. In fact, during my childhood one of the rules in our family was, "what goes on in people's homes is their business." I heard both my parents make this statement, and it became the law to me, especially in regard to what happened in our home. Even as I grew into adulthood and started to grapple with the effects of the abuse, I could still hear my parents' voices reminding me to keep silent. So when my aunts started to ask me questions, I felt that either my father had not told them about our rule, or they had decided to break it. They were ready to listen; I was not ready to talk. There was a part of me that believed I still needed to protect the reputation of my father, the brother my aunts so loved, and even the reputation of my mother, although I hated what she had done. It is ironic and strange how a person who is abused can so easily turn into a protector of the abusers.

At the same time I was pretending that everything was fine, I often engaged in the technique of "cut and run." When I was questioned about my childhood, even if it was by someone with only a casual curiosity about my estrangement from my family, I made it clear that the topic was out of bounds. Often, my distorted thinking led me to believe that the person who asked me somehow wanted to obtain some "secret" information that could be later used against me. If I convinced myself this was true, I cut the person out of my life, no explanation given. I now understand the irrationality of these thoughts and of the resulting behavior. And I also understand the reasons for it. As a child, my trust in the people closest to me had been broken so often that when I became an adult I trusted very, very few people.

As I began living and working outside of the isolated world of my family, people began to inquire about my life in an attempt to get to know me better. The more these inquiries increased, the more threatened I felt about having my past revealed, and the better I got at pretending. I recall dating a young man in college and that we became very fond of each other. One day, he started to ask questions about my child-hood and my family. Without losing a beat, I proclaimed, "I don't really remember much about my family. I lived in an orphanage." At that moment, instead of pretending that noth-ing out of the ordinary had happened in my family, I chose to pretend that I did not even have one. I was surprised when those words came out of my mouth. Later, after I realized what I had done, I knew that I would not be able to sustain that particular lie, so I broke up with him, and I did not use that fabrication again.

I also pursued another method of pretending. I scheduled my life so that it appeared orderly and perfect. I thought if it looked fine, it would be fine. Continuing the habit I had developed in college of constantly staying busy, I spent every spare minute I had working and being involved in a variety of activities. I was the president of the Minneapolis chapter of a national accounting association, the leader of a women's accounting group, a volunteer for the Big Sister Program, I took courses in art and writing, and I socialized with other employees at the CPA firm. I had no time left for becoming more aware of who I really was or why I acted as I did. The truth of the matter is that I crammed as much stuff into my life as I could not only so that it would look good, but also so I did not have to think about the things that I found painful. Although I could not have verbalized it at the time, I was not yet ready to look at the experiences I had many years before, experiences that, despite my efforts to pretend otherwise, I was still carrying with me.

⊱ STRIVING FOR PERFECTION ⊰

Trying to give up the need to be perfect has been a lifelong struggle for me. I have come to understand that perfectionism is yet one more way that I pretended. I believed, or rationalized, that nothing could be wrong with someone who always performed perfectly.

I began my quest for perfection as a young child in school, in an attempt to be acknowledged and accepted for something, for anything. Except for the few months in high school that I devoted myself to rebelling, I was a stellar performer. This included my academic endeavors and any of the other activities I took on, whether it was cheerleading, being the editor of the school paper, or participating on the public speaking team. My obsession with being perfect continued throughout college, where I drove myself to spend hours and hours studying to pass the CPA exam while I was a junior and to graduate first in my class in three years. During the moments of recognition that followed achievements such as getting a perfect score on a test or an A in a classes or winning a school competition for a project, I felt like "somebody."

As I reflect on it now, I can see that what I was actually doing was driving myself hard in an attempt to receive the attention and acceptance from others that I had never received from my family. And because my self-esteem was so low as a result of my treatment during childhood, whatever acknowledgement I got from my achievements only felt good for a moment and then I was plunged into insecurity and feeling the need to prove myself all over again. No matter how perfect I was, it was never perfect enough to make me feel that I was an acceptable, let alone lovable, human being.

❧ THE "PERFECT" JOB ❧

Having never felt safe as a little girl, I craved security now that I was an adult because the little girl aspect of me felt starved for it, so I chose a career where I could earn a comfortable living. Given my desire to stay busy, my career had the added bonus of an 80-hour work week. There were other added benefits—perfection was expected of everyone, and mistakes were not tolerated. Employees who made mistakes were judged harshly and often humiliated in front of others. This environment felt very familiar to me, and I thought I had hit the jackpot!

As I mentioned, I got this job when I graduated from college. It was 1969 and the federal government was starting to pressure the then "Big 8" international accounting firms to integrate women into their workforce. The medical and legal professions had undertaken this effort without political pressure, but the large CPA firms were holding on to their practice of being good ol' boys clubs. When they finally yielded to outside influences, I was one of three young women hired to work as accountants in an office with about 250 men.

Most of the 50 new male recruits accepted, or at least tolerated, the women on the accounting staff, as they had been exposed to us in classes during their university training. The senior and middle-management members of the firm were not so thrilled. The rumor around the water cooler was that the older partners wanted it known that we were employed with the firm not because of our education or talent but only to pacify the growing women's movement. Management extended professional courtesy toward us, yet there was also an air of subtle contempt when we engaged with them. I sensed this, but I did not care. I had my own agenda and my own plans for success, and I was going to do whatever it took to succeed at the firm. I was going to become the first woman audit partner in the office.

At that time, sexual harassment was not against the law, it was standard practice, and if you were a woman, accepting it was a job requirement. To one extent or another, all of the women staff members at the firm—accountants as well as secretaries and bookkeepers—were harassed. It was a fact of life. It was known to upper management, practiced by some, and it was not discouraged. A woman who wanted to rise to a management position or retain her job was at a severe disadvantage if she thwarted the advances of a person in power. In spite of this atmosphere, I was able to prove myself to the firm and to climb the proverbial corporate ladder. I attained the position of supervisor, then manager, and ultimately began the process of admittance to partnership.

Then one day, at a partners' meeting, the senior managing partner of the office announced that the first woman audit partner would not be coming out of his office. Unbeknownst to me, he had made an arrangement to trade me (like a ball player) to the New York office, where "those liberals" were willing to take the risk of admitting a woman audit partner to the firm. When this plan was explained to me during the partner interview and investigation process, I decided to resign from the firm and go into private practice. I did not want to move to New York, and I did not want to be sold like a piece of meat. In retrospect, I am thrilled that this chain of events occurred, because the life of a partner in an international accounting firm is all-consuming. If I had continued on that career path, it would have made it harder for me to recognize how desperately I needed to acknowledge and deal with the abuse I had experienced, and to understand how it had contributed to my becoming the unhappy, high-achieving person I had become.

This job had provided the perfect opportunity for me to direct my pent-up childhood anger about men towards my male subordinates. The attitude at the accounting firm was that staff members were expendable commodities, so supervisors and managers had free reign on how they treated them. As I rose up the ranks, I seized the opportunity to show the men working for me that I was the boss. I used this power to express the anger I could not show as a child. The anger I displayed at this job became, in effect, a delayed reaction to my father's neglect and my brother's cruelty.

It was not until I left this world that I was able to take a hard look at the overly aggressive management style I had acquired while I was with the accounting firm. I had climbed and clawed my way to the top. My mentors were all male, so I learned how to act like a man in this man's world, and to play by rules that were made up in the men's locker room. The use of raw power was new and intoxicating to me. I had wielded my power over others like a sword, I had been arrogant, and I had lacked sufficient compassion. Luckily, I learned about a much kinder way of running a business when I left to work as an executive for a large travel company, which conducted itself in a much gentler manner. I discovered that I did not have to be harsh with people to get the job done. It was amazing to find out that encouragement, support, and compassion resulted in a much more effective management style.

❧ THE OVERPASS ❧

Having never had the opportunity to play as a child without the looming threat of some kind of punishment, I wanted to play freely when I became an adult. I tried to satisfy this desire by letting myself have as much alcohol as I wanted.

I was 21 when my sister, two years my junior, decided to get married. I managed to get drunk at my parent's house when we made a stop en route from the church to the reception. I did not make it to my sister's party, so I am assuming I had my own celebration. This remains a pathetically embarrassing memory for me even today. What is even more remarkable is that no one said anything to me about my behavior. It was one of the things that you "just didn't talk about" in my family.

During my twenties, I started drinking more and more. My friends and business associates were also heavy drinkers, so there was no gatekeeper on the liquor cabinet in my life. At times, I thought my consumption was "a little out of control," and I would pride myself by not drinking for two weeks, just to prove I could stop. With that ability demonstrated, I would return to my old habits. An exceptionally bad hangover or a near-miss car accident usually pushed me into temporary sobriety—until I was able to blot out the memory of those events. These feeble attempts to prove to myself that I was not addicted to alcohol were part of my denial of what was actually transpiring and of the fact that my life was not in my control. The predisposition to alcoholism based on genetics and my environment was winning the contest, and I had become what I said I never would be and what I so despised.

On the eve of my thirtieth birthday, while I was working in the travel business, I was partying at an after-hours club. Four of us were gathered there—me, my vodka gimlets with hazelnuts, my boyfriend, and his manhattans with maraschino cherries. Our choices of drinks reflected the sophisticated, important businesspeople we thought we were at the time. We made yuppies look bad before that term was ever invented! A late dinner included drinks before the meal and for four hours afterward. That night, my boyfriend and I were totally wasted as we left the bar around 2:00 a.m. We had arrived at the restaurant separately as we had both come from our offices, and we got into our cars and went our separate ways, my boyfriend having an early-morning meeting. I was a little perturbed that I did not get a birthday present at dinner. I did not realize that my gift would be arriving very soon.

It was mid-April, and Minneapolis was blanketed with snow from a storm. I entered onto the freeway, heading for my home ten miles away. In my drunken haze, it took a while before I figured out why the headlights in my lane were coming at me. I had entered the exit ramp of the freeway and was traveling in the wrong direction.

At that moment, something outside of me took over the situation. I remember my car being pulled over to the right side of the road, and stopping on the shoulder of the freeway. I got out of car, leaving the engine running and the driver's door open. I walked in front of the car, past my glaring headlights to the railing, and dropped to my knees in the snow and melting slush.

In those days, God spoke to me in a much more firm tone than we converse in today. I clearly heard a voice say, "If you want to kill yourself, asshole, jump off the bridge. You can do what you want with your life, but you have no right to take anyone else with you." I remember standing up and looking down to see how far the drop was. I do not remember at that moment consciously making a decision to live. In fact, I remember nothing else for the next several hours.

Unlike my grandfather Frank Witte, I did not wind up killing myself in a drunken stupor on a road in the early-morning hours. That was not my destiny. I woke up the next morning in my bed, my car in the garage. I do not understand how I got there. What I do know with absolutely certainty is that I have been sober every day of my life since that night on the bridge.

If our destiny includes the potential to learn certain lessons, I believe that the circumstances we need for that teaching will appear in our life. When such an opportunity presents itself, we may not respond to it the first few times. Sometimes we ignore the messages forever and miss the chance to grow. If we are fortunate, we will pay attention, and our life will be eternally changed because of what we have learned. This is what happened to me on the shoulder of that freeway overpass.

I made the choice to stop drinking, when I arrived at one of the many great forks in the road of my life. Make no mistake, the day I stopped drinking was only the first day of my recovery. For me, that road is one I will travel forever. The decision I made on that freezing night was a great gift to myself. Afterward, without alcohol dulling my emotions, I was forced to look at the world and at myself with much clearer vision. And by the grace of God, this happened before I married and had a child.

⮞ MEN AND MARRIAGE ⮜

As I grew into a young woman and began social interactions with men outside of my family and community, I did what a lot of children raised in abusive and alcoholic environments do—I recreated the abusive environment. The men I chose for relationships during my twenties fulfilled my unconscious need to be treated as if I was as unworthy as I felt. Most of the men were alcoholics, emotionally abusive, and unable to commit to a relationship or to themselves. They were also suave, charming, and brilliant, which added to my fatal attraction to them. The combination of their flaws and my damage created a combustible affair.

I often turned these relationships into a power struggle as I tried to control men with sex. I told myself that I had the power because I offered the sex, but in reality, I confused sex with love. Since I had a great need to be loved, it was actually the men who were controlling me. Until I was able to identify this pattern of relationships in my life, I repeated it over and over. Even when I told myself I was going to pick a better partner for myself, I always attracted the same type of man. I had not yet begun any significant therapeutic work on myself, and without it no vow that I made to choose a better partner changed the view I had of myself of being unworthy and unlovable. My lack of self-esteem came through, no matter how successful I was, no matter how well I dressed, no matter how powerful I appeared. There was always someone just as dysfunctional as I was, who was attracted to my internal damage and my self-defeating behavior, and invariably I would find him.

One of my long-term relationships during my twenties was with a man who possessed all the qualities that I admired at the time: intelligence, charisma, and power. And by the way, he was married. He was "in the process" of leaving his wife during the entire five years we were together. We talked about the idyllic life we would share together when he was free and available. Even as unhealthy as I was then, I knew he was lying, and I knew I was lying. Some part of me understood that the fantasy world I had created was based entirely on falsehoods and untruths. On the other hand, I believed this relationship was just what I deserved, and it was definitely what I knew. I grew up in a world where I did not trust men, and what better way was there to prove it than by getting involved with an adulterer? I thought it was natural to be isolated from the people closest to me in my life, so why not find a relationship that could never be complete and that I could never be open to other people about? I associated love with abandonment, so it made perfect sense to seek out a man who would definitely leave me. And I added to my sense of unworthiness with the shame and guilt I felt about the affair.

Today I realize that back then I had no understanding about what was involved in a healthy relationship and no tools to establish one. At that time, I was emotionally damaged from the trauma and pain of my childhood and under the influence of alcohol. And I had no comprehension of any of this. I brought into my life the type of relationships I believed I deserved, and I did this until I stopped drinking.

Fortunately, I began my healing work when I turned 30 and I became sober. I would have had no chance of a entering into a healthy relationship without doing so. A year into my sobriety, I met my soon-to-be husband, Paul. He was the polar opposite of the men I had previously been involved with. He was kind, gentle, and supportive, and he absolutely adored me. He did not have an alcohol problem, and intuitively I knew I could trust him not to abandon me.

Even though I had stopped drinking, huge parts of me were unhealed when I married, and I had not yet begun or even recognized the need for a program of abuse recovery. My lack of self-esteem caused nagging thoughts about what was going to make our marriage come to an end, even though I knew Paul had meant it when he had vowed "until death do us part." In the world in which I had grown up, noth-ing good lasted very long, and concern about my marriage always lingered in the back of my mind. I was also not at a point in my life where I understood real intimacy. I com-mitted to my marriage as a partner and as a future parent, yet I do not believe I was involved in it with my entire heart and soul. During my marriage, I never spoke to my husband about my childhood experiences, so our relationship was not based on genuine openness. I did not comprehend this at the time, yet I understand it fully today. I worked at making our marriage good, and it was good, yet it was never great. I take responsibility for this, as I was not healed enough to believe that I deserved anything great.

❧ LEARNING TO PARENT ❧

A year into my marriage, I was surprised to find out I was pregnant. My husband and I were on vacation in Italy, and I thought I had picked up some travel bug in Milan. I got sick enough to need medical attention, so Paul took me to the emergency ward of the local hospital. There I was treated with antibiotics and told to see my doctor in the United States upon our return. I did that, thinking my doctor would confirm the diagnosis and give me more antibiotics. Instead I discovered I was pregnant. Paul and his parents were elated. I was in shock and slightly panicked, and I questioned what kind of mother I would be. Intuitively, I knew that if I did not get some insight into myself and my background, and how it might influence my ability to be a good mother, this new job I was about to take on could end in disaster.

Many of the pregnant women I knew ran to the bookstore to buy a copy of Baby and Child Care, by Dr. Benjamin Spock. I, on the other hand, went looking for information about the effects on parenting when you have a background of being abused as a child. All the professional literature agreed that the odds overwhelmingly favored repeating the cycle of child of abuse from one generation to the next. Initially, this terrified me. After I calmed myself down, I knew that once more I needed to "rise to the occasion," something I was used to doing when faced with a challenge. I read books about parenting, I watched videos, and I spoke with parents whose parenting techniques I respected. And as the grace of God works, I was provided with some excellent role models to help me with this monumental task.

I was truly blessed to have married into a wonderful, loving Italian family. Even today I smile at the irony of my father saying to me when I was a little girl, "Marion, if you can't be an Italian, then marry one." I wonder whether this was a premonition on his part, or if I turned it a self-fulfilling prophesy. Either way, it was a good decision.

Paul, an only child, was extremely close to his parents, Angelo and Catherine Scaletta. When he and I got married, his parents told us that if we ever moved anywhere warm, they would follow us. I heard them make that statement more than once, and I thought, "What a nice thing to say." I did not believe that these people would forego everything they had in Chicago, the place they were born and raised and had lived their entire lives. When our daughter, Angela, was two years old, Paul and I moved from Minneapolis to Palm Springs, California. Six months later, Angelo and Catherine sold their home, said goodbye to the snow, and relocated a mile down the road from us in sunny Palm Springs. I learned a lot about family love and commitment from them.

I also discovered my parental mentors in them—they were the gold standard according to which I parented Angela. I observed them and the way they interacted with their son. They maintained a balance of caring and concern, they established appropriate boundaries with him, and always, always gave him and me and Angela lots of love. My daughter was a very lucky little girl. She was a princess in her father's and my eyes—but she was a saint in theirs!

I recall a very simple incident that occurred at my in-laws' house and that had a profound influence on me. Angela was around three, and she had spent the day with grandma and grandpa. When I arrived to pick her up after work, she was playing in the family room with her toys. The family room's sliding glass doors were locked so that Angela could not get outside, as there was a swimming pool in the backyard. This did not deter my toddler from trying to get out by pushing on the glass, leaving a series of small handprints, some of them bearing the remnants of whatever she had for lunch that day.

Both the Scandinavian and German sides of my family prized cleanliness. In our farmhouse, it was very important that everything be clean, proper, and in its place, and I brought this attitude into my housekeeping. Therefore, my eyes immediately spotted the handprints on the glass, and I asked Catherine where she kept the Windex so that I could clean the sliding glass doors. She quietly and firmly told me, "Don't worry. I like them there." It took a great deal of restraint on my part to leave her house, knowing that the glass was dirty and that I had left it that way.

The next week, we were at Catherine and Angelo's house again, and I spotted some handprints on the glass. I asked Grandma if those were the same ones from the week before. She looked over to me, smiled, and said "Yes." Angela eyed the glass, and her eyes became wide with delight that her "artwork" was still present. My in-laws were no slouches when it came to cleaning, although they were not as compulsive about it as our family. I was surprised that the glass doors had not been cleaned, so I boldly asked, once again, if I could clean them. Catherine sighed a little and said "Marion, I like the handprints there, and when I am ready to wash them off, I will." Then she said, "Do you realize that those little prints are unique, that your daughter's hands have already changed, and she will never make another set like them again?" I did not respond, as I was not sure what to say. I was a little stunned; this type of thought process was foreign to me. During my childhood, clean windows were always more important than children.

My mother-in-law's comments provided a deeply important "teachable moment" for me. In all honesty, I never attempted to become as patient a mother as Catherine had been. But after that day, I became a little more patient than I had been before, and that was a good start.

Raised by wonderful parents, Paul was a wonderful father. He adored his little angel, and spent every hour he could with her. I had a more demanding work schedule than he, and I often worked late. Many times I came home well after they had eaten dinner. It would be heartwarming to see him asleep on the couch, our sweet baby girl sleeping on his chest, heart to heart. I did not realize it at the time, but I believe I was jealous of the gentle, natural way my husband interacted with our daughter. He instinctively knew that all she really wanted was love, whereas I tormented myself to make everything in her life was "perfect." I took her to the doctor for the slightest sniffle, and I made sure the curtains in her room matched the Holly Hobby blanket, sheets in her crib, and mobile! I childproofed the entire house and kept it spotless. My personal standard for cleanliness was achieved when I felt that emergency brain surgery could be performed in any of the bathrooms at any time. A part of me felt too inadequate to be a good parent, so I tried to compensate by at least making sure that everything in my daughter's life looked perfect to the outside world.

In spite of my deep-seated feelings of parental inadequacy, my husband and I developed a system of co-parenting that worked effectively for us and for Angela. He was more lenient and much more patient than me, and I tended to be more firm and very protective. We were unified on all major decisions, even though our styles of reaching a decision were very different. He took a long time to deliberate, and I was accustomed to making choices on the spot.

Although my in-laws were a huge influence on how I raised my daughter, a lot of my parenting was on the fly, and many of the decisions I made revolved around doing things in the opposite way from my upbringing. I freely admit that I was overly protective of my little girl, and I went overboard to make sure she did not get into any unsafe situations. I now realize that the "reverse-modeling" method I employed was flawed, since in large part it was based on my belief that the world is not safe. At that time, I believed raising Angela in the way I did was the right thing to do, for I took my job of keeping her safe and protected very seriously. I understand more clearly now that children learn from all types of experiences, and as parents we cannot keep them safe from all harm, no matter how well intentioned we are or how hard we try. I have come to understand that one of the keys to appropriate parenting is finding the right balance between holding on and letting go, and knowing the right time for each.

Indeed, parenting was a very challenging job for me. A major reason for this was that I had to raise two children at the same time. One was the daughter I gave birth to, and the other was the child-like part of myself. Because the wounded little girl inside of me had not been adequately parented, I was unable to call upon that aspect of myself for guidance as I parented my daughter. During my pregnancy, I had some awareness of this, and that is why I started the process of investigating how my childhood abuse might affect my parenting abilities. But it was not until I began therapy in my forties that I seriously dedicated myself to the process of re-parenting myself—giving the wounded, child-like part of myself those things that I had not gotten from my parents, such as nurturing, affection and recognition.

❧ WHAT ABOUT NORTH DAKOTA ❧

Before my marriage, while I was establishing my career, my visits to Fargo would be infrequent and usually revolved around the holidays. My brother and sister had each married and had small children, and I enjoyed seeing my nieces and nephews grow up. During these short trips, I would remain very secretive about my life, and I shared little of my work success stories with my family. I believe I did this as payback to my parents for not supporting me during college. I was not going to give them anything to brag about with their friends, as I felt they had played no part in my success.

Still, I was able to enjoy my father's sense of humor and to carry on lighthearted conversations with him. My mother and I had an extremely stilted relationship. We spoke very little, and when we did it was about nothing of consequence. At that time, I had not fully acknowledged to myself how angry I was at her, but the tension I felt brewing beneath the surface was enough to make me avoid discussing any subjects that I thought would result in some type of emotional upheaval, either on my part or hers. My childhood was definitely a taboo topic for me and for her.

Aside from these visits, I would telephone my parents to acknowledge birthdays and Mother's and Father's Day. I do not recall that they ever called me. The lie I had told years earlier about being an orphan had a lot of truth to it.

A year after I met Paul, he and I became engaged, and he accompanied me to Fargo to meet my family. It was a pleasant trip for me, as everyone spent time getting to know him, and they immediately became very fond of Paul. The entire family attended our wedding in Minneapolis a year later. Paul and I visited North Dakota two or three more times before we moved to California. I found it interesting that I felt much more comfortable in the old "tribal environment" when Paul was with me. I felt safe and supported, knowing that I had somebody by my side that was totally in my camp. This was a new feeling for me, and I liked it.

After we moved to California, Paul would occasionally ask if I wanted to go back to North Dakota for a visit. I would always say no, and he never pushed the issue with me. As I watched Angela grow, I started thinking about my own childhood, a place I had not wanted to revisit, either physically or emotionally. My desire to keep Angela safe from anything resembling what I experienced became an obsession with me, and part of my fixation on protecting her including keeping her away from North Dakota. Paul and I agreed to include a provision in our wills granting guardianship to Paul's mother and father in the event that something happened to us. We also included clause, which I added, that she not be allowed to have contact with my parents. I understand how irrational, almost insane, this action appears today. Back then, it made perfect sense to me. I had become a warrior mother, and my job was to defend my daughter, even after my death.

As my parents got older, they would spend a month in Nevada during the winter to escape the bitter North Dakota cold. On their way to Nevada, they would visit us in California, and that gave them the opportunity to see Angela. They liked

Angelo and Catherine and would spend time at their home. Paul enjoyed my mother and father, and the feeling was mutual. He had a talent for making people feel very comfortable, so their visits were congenial. Before they arrived, I would get apprehensive about their visit, hoping that my mother and I would not fall into old habits and get into a disagreement. I mentally prepared myself to be on my "best behavior" so that we did not get into an argument, and much to my relief, I never started one and neither did my mother. My relationship with her on these visits was cordial, much like when I returned home during college. I treated her and my father as well as I would any guests in my house. The fact that we never got involved in conversations about my past or my childhood made our visits more enjoyable, although I was only masking my true feelings, which would be coming to the surface in the next few years.

In the end, I wound up being glad they had come to see us and they had gotten acquainted with their granddaughter. By this time in my life, I had reached at least some understanding that my daughter's relationship with my parents did not have to be the same as mine had been. I wanted them to know what a great kid she was, and I also wanted Angela to know that she had other grandparents in addition to Paul's parents, with whom she spent so much time. I watched my parents' interactions with her carefully, and I can truthfully say that they showed her great affection.

Although they never expressed it directly to me, I could sense that my parents were impressed by the life I had created for myself. I had a comfortable lifestyle and a husband who loved me, I was raising a terrific daughter, and I was totally supported by my in-laws. I did not need them to say how proud they were of me, as I no longer sought their approval. But I would soon discover that I was not as healed as I thought I might be. A few years later, much to my surprise, I would find out that I was still concerned about disappointing them. And when I started a serious path to recovery, I would come to fully understand how angry I was at both of them.

❧ HAPPILY EVER AFTER ENDS ❦

In my late thirties, five years into my marriage, an unsettling feeling started to permeate my entire being. My duties as a wife, mother, and business owner were not as fulfilling as they had been in my early thirties. A feeling of unfinished business was washing over me, and intuitively I knew that it was time for me to begin an exploration of the past that I had been denying for so long. I sensed this process would involve a lot of healing work and that major changes were going to occur in my life. My inner guidance told me that I needed to take this journey alone, without my current family.

I stayed in my marriage five years after these feelings began. I had a lot of reasons for doing so—some admirable, some not. I did not want to hurt my husband. I did not want to hurt our daughter. I did not want to hurt my in-laws. I did not want to disappoint my parents. I did not want to give my family a reason to judge me. I did not want to have a "failure" on my record. I did not want to have people realize I was not perfect. And part of me was afraid to leave the most supportive relationship I had ever known, and to journey into unknown territory. For those five years, I agonized over these reasons, usually one at a time, sometimes all at once. My foremost thought was about the effect of a divorce on Angela. I had faithfully protected her from all the harm that I could up to that point, and now I was going to inflict pain on her. At least that is what I was sure would happen.

During this period of uncertainty I did manage to engage in an activity that diverted my attention away from these nagging thoughts. California real estate values were escalating during the early-to-mid-1980s and many people were making money in this lucrative market. I decided to enter the field in 1986, using the money from the sale of our house in Minnesota to purchase nine acres of land in the Palm Springs area. I formed a real estate development company and entered into a partnership with a general contracting firm to build the first twelve houses in a twenty-six home community. I will sum up this venture very succinctly—things did not work out very well. By 1988 the real estate market was at the beginning a turbulent decline, and eight of our homes remained unsold. We were unable to meet the construction loan obligations, so the bank took the project back. I put my development company into bankruptcy and was left with the personal debt from the funds I borrowed to get into the business. My foray into the exciting world of real estate development turned into a nightmare, and my business became one of the many casualties of the financial crisis in California in the late 1980s.

Initially, Paul was supportive of me going into this venture, and he agreed to ask his parents to loan me money to fund the development business. When it failed he was less compassionate. I had placed our financial security at risk, and had lost the gamble. The guilt of my business failure only added to the guilt I felt about wanting out of my relationship. It was this at this time that I asked Paul for a separation.

Paul was taken off guard by my announcement, although he was aware that we had been growing apart. He and I had developed separate interests by this time, Angela being our common bond. He requested that we go to a marriage counselor, which we did. This proved to be of little help, even from the beginning. When the counselor asked what we were both looking for, Paul responded that he wanted to make our marriage work. I said I wanted a divorce. I think the counselor figured out pretty early on that the odds were against us. We separated shortly thereafter and filed for divorce within another two years.

My decision to leave Paul was a huge surprise and disappointment to everyone in my life, and I could offer no acceptable reason to satisfy their need to know why I had made this choice. My husband, my daughter, and my in-laws, the people in the world who loved and supported me more than anybody, were upset and devastated. Angela was confused and torn by the fact that the parents she loved were no longer together. Paul was hurt and disappointed, and became depressed over it. Yes, I created a real mess.

There were many days when I questioned if I was doing the right thing. It took strength to remain firm in my resolve that this is what my soul wanted and to stay rooted in the knowledge that I needed to follow my spirit's heeding. That same knowingness inside of me that I had relied on when I was a little girl was now leading me on a new journey, to reclaim parts of myself that had been lost long ago.

As I now think back to those days, I understand that there were additional factors in play that led to the actual ending of my marriage. My business failure added to my low self-esteem, which was the source of my belief that I was not able to maintain a loving relationship. I also realize that my tendencies towards self-sabotage strongly influenced my actions at that time. I can see all of this more clearly today, as I now have the ability to connect some of these dots. But, no matter what all the reasons were, and even if I did not understand everything at the time, I firmly believe I was destined to take the course of action I did.

And so painful as it was to everyone, after ten years of marriage, I left my husband for another person: me.

My husband and I separated when Angela was seven years old and divorced when she was nine. We both knew that the divorce would be difficult for her, since she was devoted to both of us. We agreed to joint custody, with no formal allocation of days or visits. We let Angela have a strong voice in the decision about which of us she stayed with on what days, and we coordinated our carpooling and school activities around this schedule. Thursday nights belonged to Grandma and Grandpa, and she stayed overnight at their house every Thursday for seven years, until she went to high school. My relationship with Paul's parents healed in a relatively short time, as they continued to care for me as the mother of their beloved granddaughter. We became cordial and friendly, although we were never as close as before the divorce. I would tell Angela how lucky she was to have so many people in her life who loved her. She would smile, roll her eyes, and say, "I know, Mom."

During the process of separation, the one issue Paul and I were in unison about was the impact of our actions on our daughter. We agreed that no matter what difficulties or problems occurred between us, Angela would remain our priority. We agreed never to make disparaging remarks about each other to her or in front of her. We have honored that commitment for the twenty years we have been apart, and have remained friends the entire time. Paul married Kris four years after we divorced. I have celebrated holidays and other special events with them, and Paul and I still share fond memories when we get together. And we remain united in our love for our daughter.

The insights I have attained about my marriage and its ending have come with the benefit of many years of hindsight. I remain solid in my belief that my spirit was leading me out of that relationship onto a new path, and I now also understand that I had completed my work with Paul. I had learned from him what we came together to share: love, commitment, and parenting. I realize as well that there was also a major psychological factor in play in my desire to end our relationship. I have come to the painful understanding that, at the time, I could not feel comfortable unless I was in a dramatic, intensely emotionally charged relationship. Having been raised in a household with a high level of anxiety and dysfunction, those were the elements that made me comfortable in a relationship. My marriage had become too tame for me. Paul's love and trust, and his willingness to share, were just not enough for an adrenaline junky like me who still did not know who she was.

๛ THE REALLY EMPTY NEST ๛

When my daughter was fourteen, she announced that she would like to leave home and go to a boarding high school. Her reasons for wanting to leave revolved around a desire to interact with young people of other cultures and backgrounds, and also a wish to attend a high-quality college preparatory school. That is what she told me, and of course I did not believe her, for I was sure she wanted to get away from me. I asked her (over and over) if my theory was the real reason, and she kept saying "No, Mom, it's not!" As I went through the process of considering her request, I eventually reached a place of accepting that Angela's reasons for wanting to go had to do with her needs, not with my faults. Part of that process involved my realizing that her wanting to leave home as a teenager was for very different reasons than those of my Grandma Blanche, my Aunt Ruby Mae and me. Angela had lived a relatively sheltered life as an only child in a small, homogenous community, and her spirit was pushing her to start her journey at a young age. Heartbreaking as it was to let her go at fifteen, it was the experience she wanted and needed, and Paul and I agreed to honor her request.

The only requirement that her father asked of Angela was that she select a school close enough to Palm Springs for us to drive up to see her if she needed us or if we needed to see her. The school she chose was 90 minutes away, and during her freshman year, Paul or I frequently drove up on weekends to visit her or to bring her home. As she became accustomed to living on her own at the school and gained a sense of independence, she wanted to be with her friends and came home less often. We all gradually settled into the routine of occasional visits, Angela knowing that I, Paul, or Grandma and Grandpa were always willing to come up on a moment's notice if she needed us.

Having my teenage daughter go away to school had its pros and its cons. Turning my child over to other responsible adults so they could deal with her typical teenage moodiness was a blessing. But there were small daily events in Angela's life that I missed being involved with, like seeing the look on her face when she called to say she had just gotten asked out on her first date. She and I stayed in close contact on the phone and during weekend and holiday visits, and she came home every summer. When I recently asked Angela if she had it to do over, would she choose to go away to high school, she said yes she would, that it was the right decision for her at that time in her life. I found comfort in her answer, for a parent never truly knows if she has made the best choices for her child. Somehow back then, I had felt it was time to let her go. It turned out to be an easy transition when she went away to college, since by that time we were all was accustomed to her being away at school for most of the year.

I realize now that my daughter was the fourth generation of young girls in our family who left home as a teenager, yet hers was under very different circumstances. My daughter made the choice herself, based on her own sense of what she wanted and needed. Her parents fully and lovingly supported her choice, and our front doors were always wide open for her return.

❧ THE PAST COMES CALLING ❧

Major events had transpired in my life by the time I was in my mid-forties. The real estate development company I owned had been forced into bankruptcy, I was divorced from my husband, and my daughter had left home to attend boarding school. All the people and activities that had previously required my attention and made me feel important and useful were now no longer part of my daily life. I began to worry about who I would be without these people and activities, since to a large extent they represented my identity. I became panicky about my future, something I had never thought about before. I realized I was having a major identity crisis, a life-purpose crisis.

It was during the period of crisis following the collapse of my real estate company that I began seeing a counselor for the first time. I had been hesitant to begin working with a therapist, mostly due to the stigma I had attached to it. To me, only weak people who could not solve their own problems went to therapy. I also thought that only crazy people sought help. If I had known how misguided some of my thinking was and how helpful therapy would be to understanding my feelings, I would have gone much sooner!

It was difficult for me to speak about even relatively benign subjects, since I had lived a lifetime of silence. Most of my initial sessions consisted of conversations about my current life, the situation in which I found myself, and how painful it was for me to be stripped of the roles that for so long had defined me. I was alone with myself as a result of the absence of the people who had been a part of my daily life. I soon discovered that this feeling of loneliness would linger on as I pursued a program of recovery, as this type of personal journey is lonely by its very nature. I had the support of professional counseling, yet ultimately this process required me to be with myself, my wounded inner child, and the experiences of my past.

Undergoing therapy was like peeling the layers off an onion. My initial "life crisis" counseling led into working on my "family of origin" relationship issues and ultimately into focusing on my childhood experiences.

Talk therapy was a valuable starting point in my recovery and healing process, since it provided a safe place for me to speak up. When I divulged the secrets that I had been silent about for so long and that I had been so afraid to look at and reveal, the therapist expressed no judgment. She was a compassionate listener and a trained professional, and through our conversations she was able to help me gain crucial insights into myself. Gradually I began to understand that my perception of myself as damaged and unworthy was the result of the abuse, neglect, abandonment, and isolation I had experienced as a child. I had not been abused because I was damaged and unworthy—the mistreatment I had experienced had caused me to feel damaged and unworthy.

My childhood mistreatment had also affected the ways that I thought about myself and the world. The awareness that these experiences had a profound influence on how I acted as an adult was vital information. Prior to therapy, I had no realization that healing was possible, or even necessary. While in therapy, I began to connect the dots. No longer trying to deny my traumatic childhood, I began to acknowledge and feel the anger and hurt that I had been trying to suppress for so long and that came out anyway in my behavior. In therapy, I not only recognized that recovery was possible, I also set a goal for myself to commit to a path of healing.

After the failure of my real estate development business, I was without a job and without the means to pay back the substantial debts I had incurred in connection with that venture. So in 1988 I did what I said I would never do again—I went back into public accounting. I worked for three years for a local CPA, saving everything I could to repay the debt to Paul's parents. Then I borrowed enough money from a friend in Minnesota, a mentor at the national CPA firm where I had worked, to purchase a small accounting business and open my own practice.

Even though I was working long hours in an effort to build my business, I also made the time to begin examining my past, participating in several types of therapy and exploring various healing techniques. My quest led me to traditional talk therapy, hypnotic regression therapy, inner-child healing, guided meditation, and journaling. A large part of the process of my recovery involved reading self-help books and attending workshops, many of them recommended by the therapists with whom I was working. I began to practice meditation, which helped to quiet my mind so I could seek internal guidance. I found that when my mind was still and not cluttered by chatter, I was able to tap into that knowingness that I had always relied on as a little girl, and it told me what I needed in a given situation.

Some of the therapy I undertook changed the way I interacted with my daughter. Although ultimately it led to a very positive change in our relationship, initially some of my behavior was quite upsetting to both of us. As I began to more fully examine my childhood experiences, I had a crisis of confidence about how I had parented my own child. Primarily this consisted of scrutinizing all the ways I had been a bad parent and trying to remember every possible mistake I had made. My list included not showering my daughter with compassion every moment; being overly protective; missing school events to which she had invited me; spending too much time working; divorcing her father; not buying her the pony she had asked for; cutting her hair too short; and on and on.

Subconsciously, I had decided that I had been a terrible parent, that Angela could not love me, and that I was not good for her. The beauty (and the darkness) of this process was that I did it all myself. I asked the questions, gave the answers, and passed judgment on myself without getting my daughter involved. Unconsciously, I tested my theory by trying to push her out of my life in indirect ways. When she came home from school for weekends, I would criticize her for the smallest mistakes and flare up in anger when she did not agree with me. One day I actually said to her, "If you want to end your relationship with me, that's fine." She looked at me with the most horrified and hurt expression I had ever seen on her face. She told me I was crazy, and I needed to get some more therapy. Ironically, although I was getting help during this period, my demons were being released and she encountered them full blast. My behavior must have been totally confusing to her. Finally she had enough, and she wrote me the following letter:

LETTER TO MARION FROM HER FIFTEEN YEAR OLD DAUGHTER

MARCH, 1998

Dear Mom,

I want to start out by saying that you are the main influence in my life. All the advice you have given me and all the times you have listened to me have helped me so much. I want to thank you for always being there and I know you will continue to be there for me.

This is what I notice: Sometimes it seems like you get mad at me for the smallest things, things that are not worth being mad at. When I broke the clock in the hallway, it was an accident. I didn't know how to wind it and I was trying to help. When you got mad at me, I got mad at you and myself, which are not good feelings to have. Please don't stay in your room or give me the silent treatment, because that doesn't solve anything. I get madder at you and become less likely to apologize. Then I get worried when you don't come out, and I need you to tell me that you will come out and work it out with me.

This is how it affects me when you are mad at me for little, tiny mistakes: It makes me sad. I fear I have disappointed you and that you would rather be mad at me than to let me apologize and learn from my mistake. I get confused that you tell me how proud you are of me and yet sometimes hold a grudge against me when I do something wrong. I get discouraged because I feel I've done my best.

This is what I need: I need you to let me be 15 and let me make the mistakes that anyone could make. When you get mad at me, I get worried, frustrated and upset and I think about what I've done to make you so mad. I get mad at myself and my stomach hurts. Everyone makes mistakes and I don't want to feel bad when I make them.

This is what I'm going to do about it: I want us not to fight anymore and I'm willing to make an agreement. I can try to listen to you more, if you can try to remember that I have opinions too and I can't agree with everything you say. This is how I feel.

Love,

Angela

Reading my daughter's words, I felt embarrassed, ashamed, and humiliated by my behavior. I apologized to her and asked for forgiveness, which she lovingly gave. My daughter had become my teacher, and for me this was definitely one of those teachable moments. I thank God she wrote that letter.

I asked Angela if she would like to attend therapy with me, not that I felt she needed to, but because I wanted to have the therapist help me understand and, if necessary, repair my relationship with my daughter. We started with a session together, then we went separately, after which we came together again for another joint meeting. This process turned out to be an important step in strengthening our relationship. I believe it let my daughter know that I wanted things to be better—that I wanted to be better. And she learned that she had the right to be heard. The sessions I attended with Angela were very helpful for me as they provided the intervention I needed at the time, and they helped to improve the communication between us during her high school and college years.

The process that I started in therapy—peeling away the layers of the onion—continues today. It was not until I was writing this book, almost ten years after Angela wrote me her letter, that I came to fully realize the effects that my childhood experiences have had on my adult behavior. With this new understanding, I have also come to see more clearly the real basis of why I behaved as I did with my daughter.

My convoluted thinking and the self-destructive actions in my relationship with Angela are prime examples of the insidious effects of the inappropriate parenting and the abuse that I experienced in childhood. I believed I was unlovable as a child, and I carried that unconscious belief into my fifth decade of life. It made no difference that my daughter constantly expressed her love for me in the way she responded as an infant, or with the words she spoke to me from the point at which she first learned language. She wrote me poems and letters letting me know how important I was in her life.

No amount of expression of love from her was enough to overcome the self-defeating, sabotaging thoughts I carried in my subconscious. It is frightening to know I carried these thoughts for so many years, and even scarier to realize that I had no idea what impact they were having on me.

The good news is that I discovered these thoughts can be reprogrammed. I have worked to re-parent my wounded inner child. I now know that the little girl in me, who never got the love and protection that she needed, is indeed worthy and lovable. And I learned that I am worthy and lovable. I have developed faith that my daughter absolutely loves me. Today I take great pride when she tells me so, and I truly believe it. And the part of me that is still a little girl is happier too, for she knows that she is loved, for I have learned to love myself and to nurture that part of me that so long ago went unnurtured.

The journey I started toward recovery was unique to me, as is every journey to recovery. Many programs are available to assist with healing and recovery. A program may be effective for some people and not for others. Anyone who commits to his or her well-being after childhood abuse must travel a road that works for him or her as an individual. As I discovered for myself, the key is to stay with what works for you until you get the results you desire, or better yet, the results you need. A program will be effective only if you commit to it and do the required work.

❧ INCIDENT AT THE SHOPPING MALL ❧

During my process of recovery, I discovered that issues from which I had not yet healed surfaced in ways and places I never dreamed of. One of the most striking and surprising ways in which such an issue revealed itself happened in a shopping mall.

I often worked late at my CPA practice and would do my

errands on the way home. One particular evening I decided to stop at the mall in Palm Desert. I finished my shopping and was walking out of J.C. Penney, exiting through the doors that led to the center courtyard. Behind me, from inside the store, I heard a slap followed by a child's cry. That howl of pain sent my mind back to a five-and-dime store in Casselton, North Dakota.

As a four-year-old, I had strayed from my family and crawled under one of the store's wooden display cabinets. There was just enough room for me to squeeze into the open space between the bottom drawer and the linoleum floor. The slippery surface of the linoleum allowed me to slide around from side to side and watch the customers' shoes going by. After a while, I started to get hot, as I was wearing a snowsuit. I thought about sliding out when I realized that no one had found me, and I was having fun outsmarting everyone. I heard people calling my name, but I ignored them and stayed hidden in my great hiding place. Eventually I was discovered and pulled out feet first when a store clerk saw my snow boot sticking out from under the cabinet. I saw the furious look on my mother's face as she glared down at me. She screamed, "Don't ever leave my sight in a store again!" Then she struck me across the face to reinforce her words. I did not understand what I had done that was so horrible, and I was humiliated at being so publicly punished.

As I was exiting J.C. Penney, the force of this memory turned me around and marched me back into the store. Standing at the checkout counter in the children's department was an enormous woman in a white dress covered with large red printed flowers that emphasized her size. She was wearing one shoe and holding its red high-heeled mate in her hand. Beside her, his cheek reddened by the blow from the shoe, was a three-year-old boy, unsuccessfully trying to hold back his tears. The young clerk behind the counter concentrated her attention on the cash register. The woman with the shoe towered over the child and had to bend low to glower in his face as she screamed, "If you open your mouth again, I'll give you something to really cry about!"

I focused my gaze on the little boy. His lower lip was quivering and tears were streaming down his face. His eyes were focused on the floor, as though he was looking for a hole in which to disappear. The abject fear on his face was very familiar to me.

The woman ended her tirade and stood upright. She turned around and directed her attention at me. I looked directly into her eyes and then at the shoe in her hand. The woman had a solid 200 pounds over me. I was thinking about the bones that would be snapped if she decided to haul off and slug me.

I reached into a deep, dark place inside of me, and the anger I found was palpable. The part of me that controlled my emotions was overtaken by Dirty Harry, and I said as calmly as I could, "If you ever touch that boy again, I will find you and I will kill you!"

The mother and I stared at one another with a cold, hard focus. I was mentally preparing for her to physically assault me. I was unsure what form the attack would take, but I knew I could be in for a great deal of pain. She, on the other hand, seemed to sense that I could muster up the anger to fulfill my promise. She stared at me in an attempt to sense any fear. When she realized I was not going to leave, she glanced away, first at the child, and then at the young clerk. I had not contemplated how I would find her once she left the store, and she did not challenge me on the matter, but I think she believed my threat to be real.

She lowered the shoe and put it on her foot, then she turned to finish paying for her items. She turned her son so that his back was to me and I could not see his face. I stood watching them, as I wanted my presence to make her as uncomfortable as possible. It took a while for the clerk to ring up the sale, and occasionally the woman turned around to see if I was still there and to glare at me. When she finished paying, she grabbed the boy's arm and strode out of the store. As they rushed away, the little boy turned and looked at me with his sad eyes. I sensed that this was one of the few times in his young life that another human being had dared come to his defense. I wondered how it might have affected me as a child if someone had spoken up when I was being severely punished. I wondered if I would have felt less isolated if someone had intervened in my childhood, even for a short period of time. Perhaps the course of events in my life would not have changed, yet it might have instilled hope in me to know that at least one person cared.

I waited a few minutes at the checkout counter. As I was about to leave, I glanced at the cashier. She was ashen faced. I intentionally added to her misery by giving her a look to let her know I thought she was weak and pathetic. She had made a choice not to get involved, even as the blow was inflicted on that child.

As I left the store and entered the courtyard of the mall, I was struck with a vision of what the lead story in the Palm Springs paper might be the next day if events had unfolded differently. The headline might have read, "Local CPA Hospitalized After J.C. Penney Store Beating." I thought to myself that it would have been worth it.

It is difficult to know what to do when encountering adults who mistreat children, as there are no hard and fast rules and each situation is different. Every so often I think about the boy in the store and pray that he is all right. I have no way of knowing what impact my actions had on his life, so all I can do is pray that it was positive. I did what I believed was right at the time. Having subsequently attained greater insight into these matters, I would have done things differently. There are more appropriate responses than mine that can be utilized when encountering a child being mistreated in a public place. You can start a conversation with the adult, or ask if you can provide assistance, in an effort to direct attention away from the child. If the child is misbehaving, you can address him or her directly with a comment of a positive nature to divert their attention away from the negative behavior. If the child is in danger, you can call for appropriate assistance. I now see the wisdom in avoiding negative remarks or looks, because these reactions are likely to increase the parent's anger and could make matters worse.

As postscript to this story, I am much older and wiser today, yet I am no less passionate in my beliefs. No longer do I accost people in a mall or anywhere else! I take out my cell phone and call the police. I have finally learned about "appropriate ferocity."

The spontaneous memory recall at the J.C. Penney was significant, for it revealed to me that, despite the work I had done in therapy, the emotional charge attached to some of the memories of my past could easily be triggered. I decided that it was time for me to explore some other forms of healing.

ഏ MY INNER CHILD ൙

I have mentioned that a significant part of my path to recovery has involved learning to nurture that child-like part of me. I began to work on this in therapy with a psychologist who emphasized healing the inner child as a primary means of healing the adult. The concept of the inner child has been explained in a variety of ways. To me, my inner child represents that part of me that still feels like a little girl and that sometimes causes me to behave in a childlike or a childish way. Focusing on this in therapy, I recognized more fully than I ever had before that the abuse I had experienced had deprived me of what children need to be healthy. Children raised in families in which abuse takes place do not have their basic needs met for love, safety, trust, respect, and guidance. The absence of these requirements for healthy development can result in fear, shame, anger, and despair in adulthood, the consequences of not being appropriately parented. Like other abused children, in adulthood I had all of these feelings. And my unhealthy and unhealed child within was at the core of my adult dysfunctional behavior.

I must admit that when I was first introduced to the concept of healing one's inner child, I was skeptical about it. The same was true when I heard about the idea of re-parenting myself. It all seemed a bit too "California New Age" to me. Then, while reading a book on raising healthy, well-adjusted children, I had one off those "Ah- ha!" moments. I realized that it is virtually impossible to become a healthy adult if you never had a childhood. When that has happened, the very pattern of normal emotional and psychological development is disrupted. With that realization, I finally comprehended the need to get in touch with that part of me that never felt safe, appreciated, or acknowledged. I needed to reach out to that little girl still inside me who never felt loved, that little girl with no childhood.

In therapy, I began to see that during my early adult years I had been reacting to the wishes of my very needy inner child. Often this resulted in my irresponsible and childish behavior, causing a great deal of pain and anguish in my life – in my career, my personal relationships, my marriage, and my parenting. I started inner child healing work in the mid-1990s, when it was very popular, and I explored this concept in workshops and in individual therapy and it began to resonate with me. It was not until later in my healing process that I really met that child within and came to understand the need to honor my childlike needs, yet not give in to my childish behavior.

First, however, I participated in another form of therapy that helped me to understand how the experiences I had as a little girl made my inner child as needy as it was.

❧ HYPNOTIC REGRESSION THERAPY ❧

All of the childhood incidents that I have described were and are very vivid to me. During years of denial as a young adult, as the memories of these events came up, I would push them out of my mind and distract myself with whatever I was doing. If I did not dwell on them it was easier to pretend they did not matter and that I could just go on without them affecting me. As I mentioned, the first time I talked about these memories with anybody was in therapy, and discussing them became a central part of my sessions. While working with my first therapist, I discovered I was unable to recall memories during certain times in my childhood. When I was asked to talk about events that occurred at these ages, my mind would go absolutely blank, and often I would become agitated at the request.

I felt that there were emotionally impactful incidents from these periods that I just could not remember. The therapist explained that when we experience extreme traumas, our mind sometimes represses the memories, storing them in our unconscious so that we do not have to deal with the pain of being aware of them. These blocked memories affect us as much as the memories that we recall. The therapist suggested that if I could bring some of them to the surface, I would gain a greater understanding of myself. She recommended I go to a psychologist trained in hypnotherapy to unlock some of this repressed information.

The first time she recommended this, I rejected it—not because I was anxious about what I would find out, but because of reservations I had about hypnosis. I told the therapist about seeing people placed under hypnosis at the state fair and the hypnotist giving them suggestions that they perform rather embarrassing acts, such as clucking like a chicken. Underlying my concern about people clucking like a chicken was the extreme mistrust I still felt as a result of the abuse I had experienced. I knew that to be hypnotized I would have to be willing to trust the hypnotherapist, and I was not sure I could do that.

The therapist smiled as I talked about the hypnotist at the state fair, proceeded to explain professional hypnosis to me, and gave me a book to read that described in detail the process and the objectives of hypnotherapy. Ultimately, I decided to pursue this technique. If hypnotherapy could reveal memories that I was repressing, it could help me on my path to healing, and I was willing to try it.

I had two sessions with the hypnotherapist. In the first session, she asked me to close my eyes and she placed me under hypnosis using a deep breathing and slow counting method. When I was "under," she regressed me back to the age of two. She questioned me about what was happening at that time in my life. What I saw under hypnosis was similar to watching a black-and-white movie of myself. The incident that I remembered—which I described aloud as I was seeing it—stayed with me as a clear memory when I came out of the hypnotized state, and it remains clear to me today. It helped to explain something that had long troubled me and that I never quite understood.

I have a small oblong-shaped bald spot on the right side of my head over my ear. As a teenager, I remember asking my mother how I had gotten that scar. She said that I had fallen down the entire flight of stairs leading from the upstairs bedrooms to the first floor. She said I had been carrying a toy and that it had pierced my head when I landed at the bottom of the stairs. Even with this information, I always thought something was missing from this narrative. For years I had let it go, since I could not recall what had actually happened. The memory that follows surfaced during my first session of hypnotic regression therapy.

The staircase leading to the children's upstairs bedrooms was eighteen steps high. It was steep, with no handrail. The ironing mangle, a machine used to press bed sheets and other large items, was stored at the foot of the stairs. It was covered with a plastic table cloth to keep it free from dirt and dust. The wheels on it legs allowed it to be rolled into the kitchen on laundry day. After the machine was plugged in, it took about fifteen minutes for the two large rollers on the top of the machine to become intensely hot enough to use to press laundry. I am two years old and I am holding a metal toy merry-go-round as I stand at the top of this staircase. A push against my back causes me to roll down the stairs and fall all the way down to the first floor, next to the mangle. One of the metal flags on my toy pierces my skull, and I lay in a pool of blood. The shadowy image at the top of the stairs made its appearance the second time I underwent hypnosis. The figure appeared in the form of a moving shape, much like a wisp of cigarette smoke. I cannot remember who pushed me, or perhaps I do not want to.

I was not able to recall this event until my mid-forties, probably because until that time I was not ready to handle it emotionally. As an adult, and with years of therapy behind me, I was able to process this experience without experiencing the original terror or trauma.

It always sounded odd to me when my mother said that the clothes needed to be "mangled." It seemed a harsh word for a household activity. Through the surfacing of this memory, I learned what it was like for the same thing to happen to a little girl when she is pushed down the stairs and mangled by an iron toy.

❧ THE HEALING CENTER ☙

The healing techniques I employed all helped to one degree or another. The most intensive of these was a residential treatment program near Los Angeles for adult survivors of severe childhood abuse. It was also the most traumatic. One of my friends, a nurse, had gone through it and felt it had helped her tremendously.

The program at the Healing Center began with an orientation session Tuesday evening at 6:00 p.m. I had driven the 120 miles between my home and the Los Angeles area many times before, and in the worst of traffic it was a three-hour drive. This time it took me seven hours, as I kept "getting lost." My inner child already knew what was in store for us, and the childlike fear I felt was constantly causing me to misread the directions. I was three hours late for the opening meeting, and I hoped the therapist would tell me I had missed too many instructions to be able to start with the group. I was disappointed. I got to stay.

I had to fill out a questionnaire, detailing the abuse I had experienced as a child. After completing the information, the three others attending the program (a woman and two men) and I were asked to talk about why we were there and what we hoped to accomplish. I felt many strong feelings during this discussion. I felt ashamed and afraid as I spoke about some of the pain I had experienced as a child. Although I had talked about it in therapy and with the friend who had recommended the Healing Center to me, I had never talked about my childhood with other people before, and certainly not with strangers. As the discussion progressed, I sensed that the other participants understood my experience and pain, and that provided a comforting energy.

At the end of the evening, the therapist asked us to sign a "contract" with ourselves, whereby we would agree that once the program had started, we would not leave until it finished five days later. As I signed that document, my inner child started to turn into an inner brat. Despite the temporary comfort I had felt earlier in the evening, that childlike aspect of me started to think that I had been tricked and then abandoned. On the drive to the Center, I had assured her that attending this program would be a good idea, but now I was in this unfamiliar facility with three total strangers, facing five days of talking about the past. My child within sensed long before I realized it that reliving a painful childhood, even through adult eyes, was going to be as traumatic as the original experience. So through her eyes, I was being abused one more time.

I was the only participant who resided at the Healing Center, as the other attendees lived within driving distance. The first night, immediately before lights out, I was allowed to make one phone call. I dialed my nurse friend who had recommended the program and told her to "fuck off" and that I never wanted to see her again. That night I needed someone to blame for being in that place and she was very handy. I did not know at the time that it was my soul that had chosen this place for me to be.

One of the participants going through the program was a 30-year-old married mother with two small children. She seemed like a woman you would find in any suburban home in America. One of the men was a stockbroker in his late twenties, and he seemed self-assured and was friendly and outgoing. The other man was a young artist and musician in his mid-twenties. He had a bit of a hippie look about him, and his dark skin and black hair and eyes gave him a handsome, exotic appearance.

When I first met the other attendees, they seemed so normal that it made me feel even more damaged. As we progressed through the program, I came to understand that these people had their own internal wounds, no matter how "normal" they appeared on the outside.

Two therapists and an assistant facilitated the five-day intensive. The schedule for the first two days included twice-a-day group therapy sessions for all attendees. Individual counseling sessions were scheduled as requested by the facilitator or by a participant. A portion of the day was dedicated to journaling and writing exercises, and we discussed the material we wrote about in individual sessions or in group. Time was also set aside for breathing exercises, meditation, outdoor walks, and group meals.

On the third day, we got into the Center's van and were driven to a cabin on a lake, where we spent the next three days and nights.

The cabin had a very rustic feel, yet it was modern and comfortable, and the lake on which it was located was beautiful. We sat outside for some of the sessions but we spent most of our time indoors in therapy. I shared a room with the other woman attendee, and the two male participants also shared a room. There was a complete kitchen, where the assistant prepared the meals. For the participants' protection, one of the rules was that a participant was never to be alone in a room (except the bathroom). Another person was to be present at all times in case we became distressed or despondent. In addition, during the program we could not engage in any sexual activities or alcohol or drug use.

While at the lake house, the psychologists continued individual and group therapy sessions. They also introduced the technique of hypnotic therapy in a group setting, with a psychologist hypnotizing one participant at a time, the other three bearing witness and providing a support system. This process was different from the hypnotic regression therapy I had experienced prior to coming to the Healing Center. Those sessions had centered on recalling a specific event that had occurred in the past, with the goal of releasing the trapped emotions related to that one situation.

This new technique was based on the concept of addressing a broader base of unresolved childhood issues, so it was common for several past events to be brought up during the session. We were each instructed to choose a time in our childhood when negative circumstances or situations took place that we felt were never satisfactorily resolved. We also had to choose people from that time that we wanted to speak to about those circumstances or situations. Then, while in a hypnotic state, each of us was regressed to the time that we had chosen, and we were given the opportunity to engage in a dialogue with those individuals.

After the therapist ended our individual session and brought us out of hypnosis, we would discuss what we had experienced while in the hypnotic state. This provided an opportunity for the person hypnotized to describe what occurred during their process and to talk about the feelings associated with their experience. Each of the other participants also had the chance to express what he or she observed as a witness.

I was the last of the four patients to undergo this therapy. With eyes closed, I was regressed back to the time when I was four years old. I saw the living room of the farmhouse in which I had grown up, once again as if I was watching a black-and-white movie. The therapist asked me to bring my little four-year-old self into the room. It took several minutes of coaxing from me, and finally I could see this beautiful little girl peek her head out from behind the sofa. I saw her clearly in my mind's eye, even though I was hypnotized and my eyes were closed. She was dressed in clothes from the 1950s, she was barefoot, and she looked scared to death. I could barely make out her face peeking from behind the couch, although as I looked at those big brown eyes there was no doubting who she was. No amount of coaxing from me could get to her to come into the room.

The therapist asked that little girl if it would be all right to bring her parents into the room. The little girl did not answer. She remained silent, almost completely hidden behind the sofa. Then the therapist addressed the same question to me, and I said yes, it would be all right. The next thing that happened was that my father walked into the living room, in his work overalls, and sat in a chair in front of me. I proceeded to challenge him, over and over again, about why he did not protect that little girl that was me when I was little. He would not answer; instead he sat looking down at the ground, just as he had when we had sat on the furnace grate together. I told him that if he was not going to talk, he might as well leave, because that is what he always did anyway. He got up silently and walked out. As he walked away, I looked over to the couch, and all I could see of the little girl was a shock of her disheveled brown hair sticking out from behind the sofa.

The therapist then asked if I wanted to speak to my mother, and I said that I did. I looked over at the couch, and by now even the brown hair had disappeared. My mother strolled into the room and took the same chair in which my father had sat. She was cool, reserved, distant. I started the conversation, asking her to tell me why she had treated me as she had when I was a child. Like my father, she sat silently, staring at me, and did not respond. I tried to speak calmly to her but soon my voice escalated into screaming as she continued to ignore me. I felt myself getting angrier and angrier, and I stood up to grab her throat. My knees buckled and I fell to the ground, and I felt myself slipping into a dark hole and losing all sense of where I was and what was actually happening. Today, the closest analogy I can draw is that I felt like Alice falling down the rabbit hole, being terrified that if my freefall did not end I would turn into the Mad Hatter. The next thing I remember was the therapist gently shaking me and holding me in her arms, telling me that she had sent my parents away and it was safe for me to come back. I thank God she had the clinical experience to bring me back from wherever I was.

Although this was incredibly frightening, it was one of the most magnificent experiences I have ever had. I got in touch with the childlike part of me more tangibly than I ever had before, only to discover how scared that little girl still was and how important it was for me to learn to take care of her needs. Although I had stood up for my inner child in front of my parents, I knew that I had tremendous work ahead of me to fully earn the trust of that inner child part of me that was still so wounded.

The day after the hypnotic regression session, I was asked to write letters to my parents as though I were still a young child. The therapist advised me to include statements that I

wanted to express to my parents and that I had not been allowed to make back then. She instructed me to write with my
less-dominant hand, and, following this instruction, I found
my thoughts flowing onto the paper as I concentrated on the
act of moving my pencil in this unfamiliar and uncomfortable
way. I share the letters with you.

Dear Dad,

This letter is being written not by the women you know now but by the little girl you never took the time to love.

I feel sad that you weren't around to see me smile the few times I did, and

That you did not share in the immense love I had for you. (We both truly lost my childhood.

You did teach me how to laugh and how to give and for that I thank you

I love you, Dad
Marion

Dear Mom,

I am sad that your life did not turn out the way you wanted it too, but that is not my fault, as we each create our own lives.

I am sad we had to inflict so much pain on each other, but whats done is done, and I will

not allow that to happen
any more.

I am sad that you are
so terribly sick, but I
know now that staying
sick is a choice and not
a penance. I have chosen
to be well.

I now understand that
you gave me the wonderful
gift of struggle, and I have
been able to use it to become
a wonderful being. Thank you
from my own beautiful new heart

Marion

I was 45 years old when my inner child finally had her say in these letters. As I read these letters today, I realize that it is helpful to explain that the sickness I referred to in the letter to my mother was an emotional illness and not a physical one. I felt that my mother had to be psychologically disturbed to have treated me the way she did.

I was amazed to discover that after pouring out years of pain during those five days, the childlike part of me had the ability to express gratitude in these letters. Prior to this experience, I had never even associated the concept of gratitude with my feelings about my parents. And the child aspect of me from which I wrote these letters had no logical reason to feel thankful. I strongly believe that the gratitude I expressed in those letters came spontaneously from the same "knowingness" that had led me to survive my childhood and to embark on the path to recovery and healing. Somehow, deep within me, I knew that the pain I encountered in my childhood was a necessary element of my life's journey. The healing I undertook because of that struggle, and the wisdom I acquired, are integral parts of my life. My little girl had acknowledged that when she wrote those letters.

While I am on the subject of gratitude, I want to add that I called my friend the nurse to apologize for the comment I made to her. She laughed and graciously accepted my apology, saying she understood the context in which I had made the call that first night. To this day, I remain grateful to her for coaxing me into going through the program.

Although I endured a great deal of emotional pain at the Healing Center, I also obtained a great deal of clarity. For the first time in my life, I began to feel both gratitude for who I am and compassion for myself for what I experienced. The therapists advised that it was important for me to resume individual therapy immediately upon returning home, as I was in a fragile state. They also suggested that I avoid contact with my family for as long as necessary, as I needed time to process everything that had happened.

Just before leaving the Center, I recorded the following in my journal: "In writing the letters to my mother and father, and taking back what had been robbed from me in my childhood, I finally cleaned the slate with both of my parents and brought closure to our relationships." I thought this was true at the time, perhaps because of the relief of having this information out in the open, and also my deep desire to relieve my pain. In actuality, I had learned that closure with my parents was possible, an idea that had never even occurred to me before. That recognition in itself brought a sense of relief, although I had yet to actually experience that closure. I had a great deal of healing left to do, and on an emotional level, I had not even begun the process of closure.

◈ AFTER THE HEALING CENTER ◈

When I had filled out the questionnaire upon arriving at the Center, I had put a check mark next to "sexual abuse" as one of the many reasons I was going through the program. That admission was a large part of why I had felt so upset and anxious that first night. Prior to seeing the questionnaire, I had not known that I would admit to this having happened to me, and I was terrified of having to confront it. As it turned out, in my five days there, I did not confront it. I did not volunteer any further information about it, and the therapists did not ask me about it, perhaps because they felt that I was not emotionally ready to discuss it.

For years I had felt as though I was carrying not just secrets, but some awful, dirty secret, and this had contributed to my being a very private person. During my five years of therapy before going to the Center, I sometimes had brief visual memories of being sexually abused as a child, but I quickly pushed them from my consciousness, and I never discussed them with my therapists. Putting a check next to sexual abuse at the Healing Center was the first time that I admitted that I had been abused in this way as well. It was the first time I admitted it in a therapeutic setting, and it was also the first time I really admitted it to myself.

Although I did not initially make the association, I recognized the effects that sexual abuse had on me long before I began to remember the actual abuse. Besides feeling that I carried a dirty secret, I did not trust men and at times was outwardly hostile toward them when circumstances did not warrant that response. Also, I had a strong need to be in control and to be invisible at the same time. I felt different from everyone else, and I lived in my own internal, isolated world. Many of these traits were also related to my physical and emotional abuse, but sexual abuse had its own uniquely devastating effects. It had robbed me of my innocence, ownership of my body, and a natural exploration of my sexuality.

About a year after I returned from the Center, thoughts of the sexual abuse I had experienced began to filter into my mind. I recall no specific event that triggered this, but the more the thoughts arose, the clearer it became that I needed to stop denying that something had occurred. For me, the sexual abuse was more difficult to acknowledge than the physical abuse. I had repressed thoughts about it for so long, and there was so much shame associated with these memories, that my conscious mind resisted recognizing the damage that this abuse had caused. I decided I wanted to go to a hypnotherapist to help me bring to the surface any memories I needed to recall. The first psychologist I had gone to for hypnotherapy used it as one of many aspects of her practice. This time I sought out a psychologist who was an expert in hypnotherapy and who made it the exclusive focus of his practice. Through a referral, I found a psychologist who met these criteria.

Prior to my first visit with this new hypnotherapist, I decided that I would not tell him about the type of past experiences I wanted to concentrate on. If memories of sexual abuse surfaced, I wanted them to come up without his leading me in that direction. I did disclose that I had been in therapy due to an abusive childhood. I told him I felt there were memories of incidents that had occurred when I was age ten and younger that I needed to recall, but was unable to remember on my own. His method of hypnotizing me was similar to that of the first hypnotherapist, and my experience of the memories coming back was again like watching a black-and-white movie.

My session with this hypnotherapist had some distinct differences from my prior experience with the first hypnotherapist. With those, I had remained emotionally distant, I described what I saw while hypnotized, and afterward I did not have an emotional reaction. This time, I cried when I felt the pain associated with the replayed event—both the physical and the emotional hurt. I became agitated when I perceived that some impending danger was going to be recalled. I would start to shake if I became overcome with fear. I also felt different when I was brought out of hypnosis this time. I was emotionally drained, yet somehow I also felt lighter.

This was also the first time any hypnotherapy session was ever recorded on tape. After I came out of the hypnotized state, the therapist would play the tape, and we would discuss my memories and work to release any trapped emotions. This process included recognizing the feelings of fear, shame, and anger that I had suppressed. I had to learn not to be afraid of having these feelings surface and to allow myself to feel them. I had to comprehend that there was no danger in having feelings—the danger was in suppressing them. I needed to learn to honor these feelings, as they were mine to be experienced.

In my first session with this therapist, I was regressed back to three years old, and I had my first full remembrance of being molested. One of the hired farmhands put his hands under my clothes and fondled me in the barn. As an adult, I still have difficulty comprehending that an adult could do such a thing. That childlike part of me that endured the abuse still can not understand why such a thing would happen. Until that session, my mind had blocked the memory, even though I had carried the emotional pain, shame, and guilt for years and years.

At the next session, I was regressed back to age ten. A memory surfaced of being molested by the son of friends of my parents who were visiting our farm. This boy was very large for his age, and I thought he was mentally challenged because his speech was slow and slurred. (As an adult, I found out from my father that he was deaf from the beatings he had received from his father.) He was a very angry fourteen-year-old boy and I was a frightened little ten-year-old little girl when he raped me in the playhouse that belonged to my cousins. This was a memory that had begun to surface after I had started therapy, and I had quickly pushed it out of my mind because I had not wanted to think about it. The trauma of this attack was so great that I repressed the details of it for decades. After the therapist brought me out from under hypnosis, I shared with him what I remembered during the session. I could not recall crying out or trying to fight the boy off at the time. While this may seem odd, it makes perfect sense to me. I was not accustomed to fighting back when I was abused, and I probably left my body during the original experience, the same way I had left my body so many times when I was physically abused.

When I had first met this boy, I had felt compassion for him, much in the same way I did for my cousin Orlind and my classmate David. I was always rooting for the underdog. After my attack, I avoided him when he was around, for I felt that he was dangerous. At the time I did not consciously know why I was suddenly so afraid of him, as I had immediately blocked the memory. I repressed it from the time I was raped until I started glimpsing images of what had happened when I was undergoing therapy in my late-forties. It is all very clear to me now, and I understand why a boy toward whom I had always felt sympathetic suddenly seemed threatening to me. He was a threat.

While I had glimmerings of having been sexually abused before I saw the second hypnotherapist, I did not consciously remember these events before the hypnotherapy. The vital lesson that I learned from recalling and acknowledging these events was that no matter how deeply I had buried or tried to bury what had happened, nothing could cover up the remnants of shame, guilt, and anger left over from these experiences. I now understand why I had such a visceral reaction when Barbara's husband tried to molest me. At that time, I had repressed conscious memories of prior childhood sexual abuse, yet the emotional charge of these events was very much accessible. And it did explain why, for so long, I had been particularly mistrustful of and hostile to men. I saw this hypnotherapist only two times, but my experience in therapy with him was a significant step in my healing process.

After the sessions, the hypnotherapist suggested several self-help techniques I could employ to process the effects of the sexual abuse. He recommended books and audio tapes, and a workshop conducted by a psychologist for survivors of sexual abuse. Once I was willing and able to acknowledge that having been sexually abused was part of my past, I was able to begin healing its effects on my life.

❧ A VISIT TO THE SHAMAN ❧

Over the years, I had developed the practice of going into a bookstore and walking into the psychology or metaphysical sections. I would glance over the books, not looking for anything in particular, and wait until a book caught my eye. I was drawn in this way to *The Way of the Shaman* by Michael Harner, about the resurgence of shamanic healing, an ancient technique for dealing with the spiritual aspect of our physical and emotional illness. I absorbed—no, inhaled—the information in his book and went back to the bookstore to see if there were any books written by or about a shaman practicing in California. I was immediately drawn to the title and the beautiful purple, pink, and blue colors on the cover of Sandra Ingerman's book, *Soul Retrieval*. I bought it on the spot, took it home, and finished reading it that same day.

That same "knowingness" that had guided me as a child was still at work. As an adult in recovery, I was drawn to pursue a soul retrieval, even though the idea was foreign and frightening to me.

I wrote to Ms. Ingerman at The Foundation for Shamanic Studies in Mill Valley, California, telling her of my interest in working with her and asking if she was taking on new clients. She was an international lecturer with an extremely busy schedule, so I had little expectation of her communicating with me. Intuitively sensing that shamanic work was a path I needed to pursue, I had decided that if she did not get back to me I would look for another person with whom to work. I was pleasantly surprised when she sent me a hand-written note, expressing her regrets that she was not seeing new clients and telling me about a shaman in my area that she knew and would recommend to me.

I traveled along a winding dirt-and-gravel road in Joshua Tree National Park to reach an old, stucco home in the middle of the desert. Several saguaro cacti grew around the perimeter of the house, and the yard contained an immense rock garden. Boulders, medium-sized rocks, stones, and pebbles of various sizes were carefully positioned to create a mandala. Several dogs roamed freely, as there were no fences. The door to the house was already open. When I reached the doorway, I was met by a smiling couple, both in their sixties, and not of the Native American descent I had expected. They invited me into their house and offered me tea. The living room was filled with well-worn furniture, and an eclectic assortment of pictures, statues, and stacks of books. The chairs had oversized cushions and the couch was covered with many pillows. It was a very comfortable and homey environment in which to get acquainted.

The shaman described the healing process he would employ, occasionally stopping to make sure I understood what he was saying. He let me know that if I had any concerns regarding what we were about to undertake, I was welcome to think it over and come back at another time. With a kind voice, and in a deeply honest manner, he said, "I will honor and respect any decision you make to stay or to go. You need to feel safe, and you must make sure you trust me to be your guide on the sacred journey we are about to take together." I instinctively knew that this was where I was supposed to be, and that I was in safe hands.

The shaman then went on to explain that soul retrieval involves the shaman taking a journey to a place referred to as "nonordinary reality" and that his wife would be drumming as a part of this process. Next he told me, "As a shaman, the beating of the drum transports me into an altered state of consciousness. In this state, I experience realities outside of our normal perception, and it is on this journey that I obtain information to assist you with your healing." He explained that during the process, I would be lying calmly and quietly on the floor, and he requested that I keep breathing slowly and deeply. He wanted to know if I had any questions for him, and I said no. Somehow I knew that whatever questions I might have were soon going to be answered. He did not ask me about why I was there to see him or what I was hoping to accomplish.

His wife asked me to lie down on the tapestry rug, my head on the pillow that had been placed there. I did as she asked, and she covered me from the neck down with a light, soft blanket. The room was already warm from the desert sunlight streaming in the windows, so I did not understand the need for the covering. But I decided to let go of trying to control the process, and I made no comment. The shaman took his place next to me, close enough that I could feel the hairs on our arms touching. By this time, I was somewhat apprehensive. I was not concerned about the journey; I was concerned about what I might discover on it. I closed my eyes and slowed my breath. The shaman's wife began the drumming, starting with a soft slow beat, gradually increasing both the tempo and volume. After a while, I was able to focus only on the drumming, as all other sounds were drowned out, even my breathing.

I drifted into a meditative state and stayed in it during the period of the drumming. At one point in the journey, my chest tightened. I thought I was having a heart attack, and I got caught up in that fear for a moment. I settled myself down by focusing as best I could on my breathing, and the tightness cleared.

I remember hearing the sound of the drum beats getting softer and the tempo slowing. I opened my eyes when the drumming stopped, and it took a few minutes for me to re-orient myself in the room. I was ice cold, and my entire body was shivering. I was happy to have the blanket covering me. The shaman appeared to be coming out of a trance. His breathing was labored and his body was shaking as he stood up and reached for the arm of the couch. He held onto it for support, and then he sat down on the sofa. After a few moments of sitting by himself, he instructed me to get up and join him on the couch.

We sat quietly for a while, each of us drinking a glass of water. Then he took a deep breath and said, "I am going to share with you what I discovered on my journey."

He spoke of being drawn to a place called "The Cave of Lost Children." Hundreds of children were huddled together in the darkness of the cave, some of them peeking out through the opening. They had all been abandoned, and they were all frightened. They had been lost there for a very long time, waiting for someone to rescue them. He said his eyes had rested on a small girl with dark hair and large brown eyes, dressed in a dirty white dress.

I gasped as he made this statement. It brought back the memory of the time when, as a small child, I had fallen down in the dirt and soiled the little white dress I had worn to church. I also recalled the experience under hypnosis when I had seen myself as a little girl barely able to peek out from behind the sofa because she was so afraid.

In a soft voice, the shaman told me, "When the little girl poked her head out of the cave, I asked her what her name was. She said she was Marion. Then I asked her to come out to talk to me, and she moved tentatively in my direction. She stopped in front of me and began crying as she said she had been in this cave most of her life, ever since she was too frightened as a little girl to live in her house. She let me know that she was still scared all the time. I had to convince her that it was safe for her to leave with me, and that someone was waiting for her. She paused for a while, and then decided to take the journey back with me to this room. I carefully laid her on your chest, heart to heart." Tears welled up in his eyes as he finished recounting what he had experienced, and he crossed his arms over his heart as though he was still holding that small child.

When the shaman did this, I started to sob. The tears of joy, relief, and release all flowed at the same time. The tightness I had felt in my chest had occurred at the point when I had reunited with that little girl who had been in the cave. While I cried, the shaman sat in quiet meditation, allowing me the space to have my release. His wife came over and sat beside me. She put her arms around me in a loving embrace, and we cried together.

I cried for everything that I was not allowed to cry for before. I cried for all the times I had been abused as a young child. I cried for all the times I was afraid as a little girl. I cried about the cellar. I cried for the things that happened in the barn and the playhouse. I cried because I did not get to say goodbye to my Grandma. I cried for my cousin Orlind. I cried for my rabbits. And I cried longest for my lost childhood.

I learned how to really cry that day. During the decades before I went into therapy, I held my tears back. Today I cry whenever I feel like it.

One of the recurring themes that surfaced during my stay at the Healing Center was my feeling of being fragmented and disassociated from my childhood and the little girl inside me. Soul retrieval was the step that I had needed to integrate the part of me that was still the wounded little girl. It was time for that aspect of me to learn that as an adult, I would be the parent to myself that I had never had, that I would nurture and support the inner child in me by fulfilling its needs. Most importantly, I would love my inner child and all the parts of myself that for so long I had believed were unlovable.

I do not know for certain if the shamanic journey was intuitive and symbolic, or if there are other realities that individuals can access. The answer does not matter to me, for my experience was rewarding and remarkable. The information that came out of this process provided me with tremendous peace and comfort.

My work with the shaman did not end my journey to healing. The insight I gained into the effects that my childhood experiences had on me added to my understanding of myself and illuminated the path that lay ahead of me.

❧ THE TWO-BY-FOUR ❧

Oprah Winfrey is fond of saying that your messages come in the form of whispers in your ears or taps on the shoulder. A year before I decided to start on this book, a message was delivered to me in the form of a two-by-four to my head.

I had built my CPA practice into a very successful business through hard work, fortunate timing, and by routinely working 60-hour weeks. My accounting practice was demanding by nature, due to the responsibility involved in dealing with other people's money. The deadlines during the income tax season provided an additional level of stress, since the hours required to meet them were added to an already busy schedule. During the first three months of the year, my work week often increased to 80 hours.

Early one March morning, I awoke feeling lightheaded. I made it to the bathroom in time to vomit up about a pint of blood. After being rushed to the emergency entrance of the hospital by ambulance, I was placed on oxygen and intravenous injections. My blood pressure was extremely low, so the medical staff could not give me any anesthetic before they forced a suction tube down my throat into my stomach in an effort to pump out another pint of blood.

I floated in and out of consciousness for six hours. At one point, a nurse asked me if my religious views required last rites. I recall someone telling me that he was trying to get a hold of a family member. I could not remember my daughter's telephone number, one of the hazards of preprogrammed cell phones. Someone ultimately found my cell phone and contacted Angela in Los Angeles.

While all of this activity was swirling around me, I remember having two recurring thoughts. The first one was, "Dear God, I hope this is not how it is going to end." My mind was sweeping through my memories, from my early childhood up to my current situation. I recalled the pain and the joy in my life, my successes and my failures, what I had accomplished, and what I wanted to do and had not yet completed. Even as I did this lifetime review, I could not grasp the idea that it might all be coming to an end soon.

My second thought was, "Please let me stay alive until my daughter gets here." I desperately wanted to have Angela at my side so I could talk to her. I was not sure what I wanted to say, I just needed to have her by me. For many years I have believed that no matter what else I do in life, raising my daughter will always be my best accomplishment. She is a beautiful person, and we have an extremely close relationship. We still have our moments, yet there is a bond between us that is stronger than either of us. Even today, I marvel that I was able to raise a well-adjusted, loving person. She understands and accepts me, even with my foibles. I love to listen as she forewarns her friends that her mom has a sense of humor you must "acquire a taste for."

When Angela arrived at the hospital, I was conscious enough to speak to her. She looked first at me and then at the tubes coming out of my body. She addressed me in the same comic style I so often use with her. "Well, what have you done this time?" she chided. I reached out to grab her hand, relieved she was there, since I knew I was in capable hands. At that moment, I acknowledged to myself, for the first time, that our parent/child roles had reversed, and I was left to wonder when that had first started.

The internal bleeding was caused by eight open ulcers in my stomach. I received a blood transfusion, spent several days in the hospital recuperating, and went home to contemplate this experience. I had been made painfully aware that I would never know how much time I had left on this planet.

I also knew I needed to determine what had really caused me to get so desperately ill. I believed I had created this situation in order to learn a particular lesson. But what was the lesson? It was up to me to wait, be still, and listen for the answer. Ultimately, the lesson of this mysterious experience unfolded. It became clear to me that I needed to write this book about the childhood pain that had been eating away at me for so long.

❧ JUST WHEN I THOUGHT IT WAS SAFE ❧

I understand that wisdom can grow out of knowledge, and that sometimes acquiring that wisdom involves suffering. Had I understood when I began this book how much pain from my past I would have to endure to write it, I might never have started the process. I had to dig down deep within myself to find a level of patience and perseverance that I did not even know I had.

As I was writing, old patterns of thinking kept rising to

the surface. As my old thoughts about being rejected were reignited, I wondered how my family would respond to my telling our secrets. As my old thoughts of not being worthy rose up in me, I wondered if anyone would be interested in this story. As my old thoughts of being unlovable screamed at me, I wondered if readers would judge or label me based on my experiences and my history. As my old thoughts of mistrust kept telling me to stop writing, I wondered who might use this material against me. And, having tried to make myself invisible for so much of life, I wondered how I would be able to face the glare of the bright light I was shining on the subject of abuse, and specifically my abuse.

So I struggled deeply with the writing process. I replayed in my mind and heart many of my painful childhood events in order to get in touch with the emotions that even today remain attached to these memories. I forced myself to go deep into my psyche and connect the dots between what happened to me as a child and how those experiences still affect my behavior today. At times, this process of self-examination and introspection was excruciatingly painful. As I previously observed about my experiences with therapy, getting to the core of these issues was very much like peeling an onion, and it was often accompanied by a flow of tears. As I peeled away one layer, I always found another waiting for my attention. Despite the number of layers I removed writing this book, I know I have many left to peel away.

While I was writing, I contacted my brother and my sister, asking them to provide any information that they were willing to share about our childhood experiences. As I spoke to each of them I realized that, despite how seldom we talk to each other, I have a great deal of love for them. In response to my request, my sister told me that she had "put her childhood behind her many years ago" and she did not want to talk about it. She said she could not confirm my experiences because we had such separate lives. I reiterated that I was not looking for confirmation of what had happened to me, but instead wanted to know about her experiences, since both of us had lived in the same house. After a long pause, she said, "Yes, we did have the same mother." I also asked my brother what memories he had about our childhood. "You mean what happened in that house?" he asked. "Yes," I responded. He simply replied "I remember nothing." After a moment of utter silence, he went on to say that he has not read a book since he left college, but he wants to read mine. My hope is that others will want to read it too, for the idea that my story may be helpful has eased the heartache of writing it.

I offer my story to every child or adult who lives with the pain and the aftereffects of a difficult childhood. I have written this book to let you know that there is hope and there is help. It is perfectly healthy and absolutely acceptable to acknowledge that one is wounded, since it is through that awareness that healing can begin.

I know this, because I lived to tell this story.

WE ARE IN A CONSTANT PROCESS OF
CO-CREATING OUR LIFE.

Marion Witte

❧ LESSONS I LEARNED ❦

2010 Today
In the end, I cannot tell anyone how to heal from the scars caused by an abusive parent. But I can share the path I have taken. It is not a straight line. Nor does the path ever really end. But it is a journey worth taking. That, I know. And if my story spares just one child from the pain I suffered, then I will be happy, and the work I've done will have been worth it.

THERE IS A BLESSING AND AN
OPPORTUNITY IN EVERY SITUATION.

Marion Witte

❧ HEALING OUR WOUNDS ❧

It has taken me many years to reach my current state of understanding and acceptance regarding the events of my childhood. As I have said, I began dedicating myself to the process of recovery when I was in my 40's. There are times when I wonder what my life might have been like if I had started my journey of healing much earlier. Then I decide that is a useless exercise. I know that all I can do is start anew each day and be grateful for how far I have come.

We cannot begin to heal our wounds until we admit that we are wounded, and we begin to work on ourselves when the time is right for us. We will revisit our past when we are ready for that to happen, and we will embark on the trip "back home" when we give ourselves permission to get on that path. We start our process of recovery when we sense that in going back home, but not staying there, we can build a new future for ourselves. As I have explained, I began my process with therapy and then added self-help practices, including reading relevant books and attending workshops. Little by little, I let in more of the past and I allowed myself to experience the emotions associated with it. I reflected on how it had affected me and continues to affect me. I was amazed that the more I found out, the more I could handle.

I offer the insights from my personal experience as confirmation that no matter what physical, verbal, emotional or sexual abuse you have experienced, you can begin to heal your life. The first step for me was to become aware of the hurt and the pain from my childhood that I had carried forward with me into my life as an adult. For many years, as I have said, I tried to ignore it and just go on as if it was not there. When I went to college, I told myself it was all behind me, and I stayed too busy to think about it. When I entered the work world, I still refused to look back and I kept up my frantic pace. In college and during my young adult life I drank to excess. This was another aid to my commitment not to think about the pain and hurt that I chose to keep in some corner of my mind, where I thought it would have no effect on me.

Despite my best efforts to disregard it, my pain affected everything about me. I felt damaged. I was extremely judgmental of myself and others. I was angry, mistrustful, and fearful. All of this was a result of the abuse I had experienced, which I thought I had put behind me. I had no idea that I had a choice about how I viewed myself and the world, or that it was possible for me to feel any other way. The day I gave up drinking was the beginning of my recovery. But it was more than ten years later that I made healing my first priority, when I really let myself look back as well as forward.

It was then that I finally realized that it is not truth that will hurt you—it is the lies.

Admitting what had happened to me in childhood was the foundation for my beginning to heal. Gradually, I began to see the connection between my childhood experiences and how I viewed myself and how I acted as an adult. I began to realize that awareness could actually lead to positive changes. This process of awareness, the first step in my healing, eventually led to the second step, a level of acceptance of my injury. This step involved a great deal of letting go, a concept that is talked about a lot and that is often much easier said than done. My letting go process included extending loving kindness toward myself and toward the people who had injured me. Engaging in the process of forgiveness was my third step. For me, forgiveness meant sitting with the painful reality of my experiences and moving to the point of eliminating any desire for retaliation toward anyone.

I had often blocked or tried to block the emotions associated with the events of my childhood. Experiencing those feelings, recognizing how they influenced my vision of myself and the world, accepting that this was so, and letting go of my desire for revenge, ultimately allowed me to forgive the circumstances of my injury.

Part of my personal healing involved writing this book. The process was excruciatingly painful at times. I discovered that I had really not addressed many parts of my childhood, and I knew that I could not write openly and honestly about them until I healed them. I remembered and relived many experiences, tapped into the emotional pain that was still present, and engaged in a constant process of forgiveness. And all the while, I was reassuring the little childlike part of me that was still hurt and fearful that she was safe, that I was safe. It was exhausting and sometimes frightening. In spite of all these things, I realize that the freedom I gave myself to speak up through this book is the greatest love I have ever shown myself.

Even though our experiences vary, there is a common ground to the suffering of all of us who have been abused or raised by adults who are emotionally ill. All of us have been hurt, and all of us have had pain inflicted upon us. We also need to acknowledge that each of us has inflicted hurt or pain on others. Part of my healing included accepting the duality of my human nature - my light side and my shadow side. It is this universal quality in all of us that forms the foundation of our connection to all other people and the basis of our compassion for each other. As we each heal our self and gain further insight and awareness, we obtain a new level of understanding, and our compassion for others will grow. The best gift we can give ourselves and the world is to become the most loving and peaceful people we can be in our own hearts and in our own lives. Not only does this choice impact the quality of our life, it becomes a beacon of light that others are attracted to and that can light the way for them to find the path to their own healing.

My message for anyone reading this is that it is never too early, and never too late, to start the process of reclaiming your life and any parts of your spirit that were somehow abandoned on your journey.

Healing is a process. In my experience, it is an ongoing part of my everyday life. As situations arise that bring back old memories and responses, I need to engage myself in awareness, acceptance, and forgiveness all over again.

❧ FORGIVING WHAT SEEMS UNFORGIVABLE ❧

I have mentioned forgiveness as the third step in my healing process. I believe that true and lasting healing can only take place when it involves forgiveness. Somewhere in one of the books in my personal library I recall reading, "Forgive those things that seem unforgivable, and you will be set free." When I first read this, forgiveness was the farthest thing from my mind. I was too angry to forgive or even to want to forgive. And yet, despite this, I sensed those words were right. Intuitively I understood that through forgiveness—by letting go of the desire to retaliate—I would gain a sense of personal freedom.

As I lived with the idea of forgiveness, gradually it became clearer and clearer to me that it would help me to heal, and I found myself wanting to forgive. But this did not mean I could forgive immediately. For me, the road to forgiving has been long and winding, and in the last few years I have taken many journeys on it. Sometimes, when a memory of a trauma comes up again, I find that I have to "re-forgive." Luckily, forgiveness becomes easier for me as I get older, so my journeys to forgiving get shorter and shorter.

I have read self-help books and heard speakers on abuse who have said that we do not have to forgive the perpetrators of our abuse in order to heal and recover. But for me, forgiveness was not just an option—it was at the very core of my healing process. The various forms of therapy that I undertook were effective in healing my emotional and psychological wounds, but only the act of forgiveness began to heal my heart and spirit.

I uncovered some important aspects of myself during the process of learning to forgive. I discovered that a major reason I did not want to forgive for so long was the comfort I took in holding on to hurt, blame, and resentment. I also enjoyed the feeling of the desire for revenge. Playing the role of the victim provided powerful fodder for my ego's appetite, for it made me "right" and them "wrong."

Being the victim also helped me keep the anger I carried inside of me under control, since unconsciously I was afraid of getting in touch with those feelings. I was scared that if I unleashed my anger I would get out of control with rage. As I started my recovery, I was amazed to learn that I did not go crazy or die as I spent time getting in touch with that anger. I learned not to judge myself for being angry. I came to realize that becoming angry, and processing that anger, is a normal and healthy step in the forgiveness process, and for me it was a necessary step in coming to forgive the abuse that had had such a painful impact on my life.

I discovered that the apologies and explanations I had wanted for so many years from my mother, father, and brother were not necessary, as they had nothing to do with my ability to forgive. I finally realized that what I really needed was different from what I thought I wanted. I learned that the true road to forgiveness for me involved becoming aware of and accepting what had happened in the past. Then I could open my heart with compassion for myself and the pain I had suffered and for those who were a party to my pain. It was fascinating to find out that the people I felt had wronged me did not have to participate in my forgiveness process, since the outcome was powerful and effective even with their absence. Both the farmhand who molested me and the boy who raped me are dead now, and from the depths of my being, my only wish for them is that they rest in peace.

I discovered that when I began to forgive, I began to release the past. I finally embraced the fact that my childhood was over and that there was nothing I could do to change it. All I could change were my perceptions and my thoughts about it. And I came to understand the difference between forgiving and forgetting. The heart can forgive anything, yet the mind may still remember what occurred. But remembering an event does not have to interfere with, or contradict, the forgiving of what happened during that event, as long as we let go of any resentment attached to the memory.

I discovered, too, that there were things for which I had to forgive myself. I had to forgive myself for being smart, for being strong, for surviving, and for wanting to be loved.

FORGIVING MY BROTHER

During a rare trip back to Fargo when my father was ill, I stayed at my brother's house. One Sunday morning, he and I were sitting at his kitchen table having breakfast. We were talking about our childhood, a topic that until then we had always carefully avoided. I asked him if he recalled any events that occurred between us as young children. I asked him if he remembered our mother beating us and how she screamed at us, and he shook his head "no." I was getting frustrated and angry, and I did not believe he was being candid with me. His body was as rigid as his chair, and he could not even look at me. I asked him if he remembered the bow-and-arrow target practice in front of the hay bales. He let out a small gasp as his face took on a look of surprise. While still looking down at his plate, in a quiet but steady voice, he said "Marion, I think about that every day of my life."

I burst into tears, and the little girl inside of me screamed at my brother, letting him know how scared I had been that day. I told him, "I carried the horror of that event around for years, confused about whether I had remembered it correctly, and not even sure it happened!" My brother showed very little emotion as I yelled, cried, and broke down in front of him. At one point, he said softly, "I am so sorry I did that, and for the tremendous pain it caused you." Long ago, when the incident took place, I had no opportunity even to scream, since I had passed out from fear. And in my family, it had not been considered necessary to talk about this traumatic event. So I had carried this memory and its pain in silence. But in my brother's kitchen, I had been heard, and that was a great place to start my healing. I believe it was just as important that I had heard my brother. I listened as he delivered his apology, and I felt the pain attached to his words, pain so deeply familiar to me.

For much of my adult life, I had questioned my memories about this event. The longer no one mentioned that it had happened, the more implausible it seemed to me that it had. Sometimes I had cast the remembrance aside as a false memory. Now that the past was openly and painfully confirmed, I could begin to heal it. My life was changed that Sunday morning in that kitchen. My brother and I did not heal our relationship that day, but with his confirmation of what had occurred, and my finally experiencing the feelings that I had held back for so long, I experienced an emotional cleansing. There was a miracle, too. I acquired a level of compassion and empathy for my brother, for I saw that he had been carrying around his pain for as long as I had mine.

I have chosen not to delve back into the past again with my brother, for I no longer want to inflict any pain on him or effect any retaliation. Any further investigation into our shared darkness would be futile, for my brother remembers very little. I no longer need to discuss any past events, for I have learned what I need to know, and I have forgiven him. That is my gift to me, and my gift to him.

During much of my adult life, my interactions with my brother were based on my recalling that he had abandoned me as a child and that he was cruel to me, and because of that I made our adult relationship very difficult. For years, I chose to have no contact with him. As I gained a greater understanding of the circumstances of our lives, I realized that both of us were products of abuse, and that each of us reacted to it in our own unique way. I came to learn that angry children do angry things. Much of what happened between my brother and I occurred because there was little or no adult supervision of our activities as children on our farm. When I stopped judging what happened, resenting my brother for it, and running away from the pain, I reframed my entire attitude about my brother. As I write these words now, I break into tears, because I have come to understand that my brother's pain is my pain.

FORGIVING MY FATHER

In May of 2001, I received a telephone call from my father. He asked if I would come back to North Dakota one last time. He told me he was dying. I had received similar calls before, and they had turned out to be false alarms, so I was skeptical. This time there was something different in his voice, and I agreed to return to Fargo.

I spent five days with my father, at his hospital bed, helping him make his final transition. He talked, and mostly I listened. He apologized for not being a good father. He said he was sorry he had not been there to protect me. He told me he wished he would have done things differently. Having said what he needed to say, and before I left for home, he asked me to give the eulogy at his funeral.

During this visit, my mother and I engaged in very little conversation, as I spent most of my time alone with my father in the hospital. Occasionally, there would be a family meeting with one of the doctors, and during these sessions my mother deferred to my brother's suggestions regarding my father's treatment or the course of action to be followed. My father begged that he not be left in the hospital to die, so my brother took him home to my parent's house and placed him under the supervision of wonderful hospice caregivers, his self-medicating morphine drip in place. I was pleased that at least he was able to live out his last days with no physical pain. My father passed away two days after I left his bedside.

I had wanted my father to be my "white knight," so I had spent at lot of my life waiting for the horse and rider to appear, waiting for and wanting his approval and protection. I did not get his approval very often, and I never got his protection, so my relationship with my father was complicated. He was less than what I desired from a father, yet in some ways he was a wonderful mentor. Through the stories and parables he shared with me when we walked through the fields or on those occasions when he talked to me about a problem I had encountered, he gave me great advice—even though often he did not follow it himself. He used to tell me to "make sure your own garden is tended to before you go looking for weeds somewhere else" and that "everybody should spend all their money when they are alive, because I've never seen a U-Haul behind a hearse." Today I place my focus not on his lack of parenting skills, but instead on the words of wisdom he shared with me.

I am deeply honored to have shared in the healing work my father and I undertook. That process had an enormous impact for me, as we broke another link in the generational chain of behavior in the family. When my father passed away, I had no feelings of abandonment as he left me for the last time.

FORGIVING MY MOTHER

Before I began the process of understanding my past and how it affects my behavior, my encounters with my mother would often trigger an angry response from me. My response was not based on a healthy, adult reaction to a situation, but rather on my interpretation of what she "really meant" by something that she would do or say. I would turn any suggestion she made into a harsh and critical attack on me, and I would fly into a rage and leave the situation to avoid any further hurt. In reality, most of the time she was just making a suggestion, but I heard it with the ears of someone who was carrying around a lot of anger and resentment toward her. I was able to listen to very little of what she said without hearing in her comment a reason to continue to be hurt and upset.

When I returned home to attend my father's funeral, two events occurred that softened my attitude toward my mother. Through these events I was able to see some aspects of her that I had never observed before. I flew into Fargo the day before the funeral, and during that time I stopped at my mother's house to visit. We spoke a bit about the funeral arrangements and about the friends of my father that she had picked to be pallbearers. I told her that Dad had asked me to give his eulogy, and then I sat and waited for her response. At the Catholic Church my parents attended, only people "of the cloth" were allowed to give a formal eulogy, so I was unsure what her reaction would be. To my amazement, my mother immediately jumped up, called the priest at the church, and told him she wanted me to deliver the eulogy. I sensed from hearing her side of the conversation that she was getting resistance. Soon I heard her say, "This is what Alvin wanted, and this is the way it will be." She hung up the phone, turned to me, and announced, "That's taken care of." I was surprised that she was willing to stand up to the priest and go against a rule of the church, and even more shocked that she won. She wanted my father's wishes honored, and nothing was going to stand in her way.

My brother came over and picked up my mother so they could attend to the final funeral arrangements. This gave me time to spend in the funeral home with my father. I needed to be alone with him. In the small, dimly lit chapel of Boulger Funeral Home, I knelt on the step in front of his casket, cried my eyes out, and said my final goodbye to my dad. I wanted to kiss him goodbye on the forehead, but I had never touched a dead body before, so I was apprehensive. I gingerly reached in and stroked his hand, feeling both the coolness and hardness of his skin, which in life were warm and fleshy. Before I left, I gently kissed his forehead.

There was something about that expressionless, quiet corpse that bore no relationship to my father who, when he was with his friends or on the steps of the church, was always laughing and usually talking. As I stood up to go, I knew exactly what I needed to do. I found a store in Fargo where I purchased a deck of pinochle cards and three red silk roses. Since visiting hours were over, I sneaked back into the funeral home and placed the deck of cards into his folded hands. I whispered, "Now you have something to do on your trip." I slipped one of the red roses under his arm, and I went back to my hotel room, exhausted and much too distraught to attend his wake that night.

The next day, a funeral mass was held for my father, and everyone attending walked past his open casket on the way to their seats. I went over to the casket, curious to see if his traveling cards had been removed, as I fully expected they would have been by a church official or someone in the family. To my amazement, the King of Hearts I had picked out of the deck and turned upward was looking right at me. I sensed someone standing at my side, and I turned to see my mother. She had a smile on her face as she said, "When I saw those cards last night, I knew it was you." Then she did something very uncharacteristic for her. From her purse, she pulled out one of my father's John Deere caps, something he never left home without. She asked if it would be all right to put the cap in the casket, to which I replied (too loudly for a church setting), "It would be perfect!" She placed it along the side of the casket, near my father's hand, and, as she did, I glimpsed the momentary smile on her face.

Standing behind my father's casket, facing my entire family and hundreds of my father's friends, I felt daunted, but I delivered my father's eulogy as he had wished. I spoke about his courage, his generosity, and his sense of humor. The prodigal daughter had returned home. At the end of my tribute, as I exited the pulpit, I walked over to my mother's seat. I took one of the two roses I was carrying and handed it to her. She was sobbing. It was the first time in my life I had ever seen her cry. I carried the other rose back to my pew and have kept it ever since.

One of the oldest adages in the world is that love can heal anything. Sometimes it can take a lot of pain to get that process started. At the time of my father's death, I was not yet ready to begin my forgiveness work with my mother, yet I could feel some of my hard feelings about her starting to soften.

My mother and I have not spoken about my childhood and the part she played in it. I have intentionally not pursued this conversation with her, and she has never brought up the subject with me. For years, I thought an explanation and an apology would make everything all right. I know now that is not true. Only I could make myself all right. I have no expectation that my mother holds the same view of the past as I do, and I am not going to seek an apology. My reason for not talking with her about my childhood experiences is that I choose not to risk the hurt of having my truth rejected, and I believe that is what would happen. I have learned that sometimes it is best to avoid situations that have the potential to inflict any more pain. For me, this is one of them.

My mother is still alive, and we work at maintaining a civil relationship. I send cards on birthdays and holidays and on occasion I call her on the telephone. This helps maintain some semblance of a connection. It is somewhat ironic that my mother was helpful to me in providing information about her family for this book. She is the last living relative that has a personal recollection of the family members in the generations that preceded me, and the only one who knows their history. She recalled what she could, and it helped to fill in some details and blank spots.

My mother was the last person in the family that I forgave, and it occurred as I was writing this book. I was surprised to discover that once I made the decision to forgive her, it happened very quickly. At some point while I was researching my mother's background, I arrived at a place of empathy for her experiences and an understanding of her human failings and why she was as she was. When I found myself feeling compassion for her, there was only one thing left for me to do. I forgave her for the behavior that caused me so much pain, and I forgave myself for holding on to that pain for so long.

My interactions with my mother, my brother, and my sister have been distant for many years. With regard to my mother and brother, I have discovered that the process of forgiveness does not always involve coming together with the people you forgive. I know that my relationships with my family could be better, yet right now they are what they are. And the place where I am currently with them is much better than where I used to be. All I can do is continue on my journey, and see where it takes me tomorrow.

❧ ACKNOWLEDGING MY INHERITANCE ❧

In addition to the three major steps that have helped me—awareness, acceptance, and forgiveness—there is another step that has proven valuable to me in the healing process. I made an effort to identify the positive aspects of my inheritance, the good things that have come to me from the family into which I was born. This included the positive qualities I have gotten from my parents and the positive qualities I have developed from surviving abuse. I had my first glimmering of this at the Healing Center, when I wrote letters to my parents. I discovered that being grateful for these parts of my inheritance has helped me to accept and to forgive. And accepting and forgiving has helped me to open my heart, to be more loving to others and to myself.

This is how I think about my inheritance today.

The Midwest farm communities of the late nineteenth and early twentieth centuries were inhabited by pioneering families whose determination and self-reliance helped them cope with and survive life on the prairie. However, the isolation associated with living in remote farmhouses dramatically diminished their access to the knowledge and information that was available in the larger world. Midwesterners of this era had a very narrow and strict view of what their world should look like. Many of them had a rigidly moralistic view of life, much of it based on and monitored by their religious beliefs. And often, they blindly adhered to the social structure and rules of the period.

Through my own experiences and through the experiences of other members of my family, like my father's sister Ruby Mae, I have learned that this type of morality can be filled with hypocrisy. I realize that not all ethical standards are loving, and they are definitely often not moral. But I have also come to understand that my family and ancestors were not ill-intentioned. Instead they were limited in awareness and experiences. They were so caught up in meeting the daily demands of life that they did not have the time to explore the issues involved in parenting and relationships. Nor did they have the awareness to understand how beneficial it would be to do so. The basic need to provide food, shelter, and a livelihood was all-consuming.

As I reflect on the cast of characters in my lineage, I am deeply grateful for the gifts they left me. I received from each of them, in one way or another, the gift of resilience as it relates to abandonment, abuse, and alcoholism. It is through our trials, if we choose to use them positively, that we have the opportunity learn, grow, and change. I also received from them the gift of strength that I needed to meet these challenges and to find my purpose and mission in life.

From my Grandpa Serum, my mother's father, I received the entrepreneurial and pioneering spirit that he used as a young man to travel across the country to learn a trade and establish his own business. I also obtained from him the knowledge that life may end much sooner than you planned. From

Grandma Serum I received the intelligence that I needed to achieve the academic and professional goals I set for myself. More importantly, I got the love and tender care she provided during a childhood so devoid of either.

From Grandpa Witte, my father's father, I received the pioneering skill that he used when he left Germany at the age of eighteen to create a better life for himself, and the pride involved in working hard and becoming successful. From Grandma Witte I received the gift of resilience, which can be accessed in the direst circumstances, and the ability to continue to love, even at times when all seems lost.

From my mother I received the intellectual capability to create a successful life, the strength to do demanding work, and the challenges she presented to me in this lifetime, which ultimately resulted in my growing to be the person I am today.

From my father, I received an understanding of compassion and generosity from watching how he helped others outside the family. I learned about the value of acting courageously, as he did in dealing with losing his eye as a child and not letting than stop him. I also got his sense of humor and a wicked laugh!

❧ UNDERSTANDING THE EFFECTS OF ABUSE ☙

All of us who were abused as children cope with its effects in different ways. Some catalogue the ways they were abused, reviewing them over and over in their minds. Some talk about their abuse with others, fueling their anger at those who abused them. Some deny the abuse, either by blocking their memories of it or by rejecting the fact that the abuse has affected them. At different times, I have coped with the abuse in my childhood in all these ways.

Many children are so emotionally devastated by the abuse

that they spend their entire lives in one form of therapy or another or in an institution. It is no secret that our prisons are filled with adults who were abused or molested as children. Other children who are abused grow up to be adults who function pretty well in society—or at least they seem to. Many achieve professional success and many marry and become parents. And many deal every day of their lives with the effects of having been abused, often without being conscious of how the abuse they endured as children influences how they think, feel, and act in the present. Until I began my recovery, I belonged in this last category.

I have personal experience that child abuse comes in many forms—physical, sexual, emotional, and spiritual. I believe that an adult inflicts abuse upon a child because of frustration with his or her life and the related emotional torment of that situation, or because of a psychological illness. Children try to learn how to react to the adult's pain so that their own pain and hurt can be avoided. I stayed out of my mother's way if she had the "angry" look on her face. If she was in one of her "good" moods, I could loosen up a bit, but never too much, as the tables could turn in an instant. For me, as for many abused children, there was never a foolproof method of avoiding pain and humiliation.

Through therapy, I have learned about the dynamics of a family in which children are abused and abandoned. I learned that a functional family is one in which the parents are there for the needs of the children. A dysfunctional family, like the one in which I grew up, is one in which the children are there for the needs of the adults. In that setting, a child is unable to establish his or her own personal, healthy identity. A baby's totally dependent status creates a scenario in which it is the center of its own universe. In an abusive environment, the child's needs are invisible to the parents, and the child gets the exact opposite of what he or she needs and desires. The long-term outcome of this situation is that the child is unaware of and disconnected from his or her own needs. It took me until

I was over fifty years old and had been in therapy for more than five years to begin to know what my needs were. And it took even longer for me to learn I was important enough to voice my needs and believe that I was worthy enough to have them met.

Parents have incredible power over their children, and children so want their parents to love them. Because of that dynamic, the emotional part of a child can believe that it is his or her fault that he or she is being treated so cruelly. This is true even if a child rationally thinks that he or she has done nothing wrong, even if the child feels that the parent is unjust or crazy, and even if the child eventually cries out at the injustice. Certainly as a child, and long afterward, I believed that something was wrong with me. I have come to understand that my perception of being damaged was based on the abuse I suffered and on my interpretation of it. From the time I was a toddler, I felt there was something inherently wrong with me, or my mother would not have treated me as she did.

I looked for flaws in myself, and when I perceived an area where I thought I was deficient, I magnified it and dwelled on it, as if that was all I was - just one big flaw. I perceived my mother's assessment that I was "willful" as a negative description of me, instead of seeing that it was natural for me to have thoughts, feelings, needs and desires of my own. I did not know that it was my birthright to want to express myself, to play, to laugh, to have the will to survive, and to have my own identity. I accepted her treatment of me as signifying that all of this was wrong, that I was wrong. If my mother was okay, I must not be okay. If I mattered to her, she was doing what she was doing to me because I deserved it. My childhood self had to go through mental and emotional contortions to hold these conflicting and conflicted beliefs and feelings. Most of this took place unconsciously and, as I have said, the effects remained with me for a long time.

I understand now that in situations involving abuse, reality may mean that Mom and Dad are not okay, and that the child may not matter, at least not in the way he or she would like to matter. Painful as it was to accept this, it was part of my recovery program.

I have talked about my father's abandonment of me. Abandonment is a form of abuse. It can occur when a parent leaves a child physically, such as through divorce or death. Emotional abandonment occurs when an adult does not give the child the support the child needs. This can happen through addiction to alcohol, as happened with my father, excessive working, or a variety of other circumstances in which the adult is emotionally absent. When a child feels abandoned, he or she has no sense of self-worth. He or she does not believe that his or her needs and feelings are important. Often the child thinks that the feelings he or she is having are wrong. And when a child does not feel safe and protected as a youngster, as I have learned from personal experience, it is a long process to restore those feelings as an adult.

❧ GROWING MYSELF UP ❧

I wrote earlier about the concept of the inner child and the need to form a loving relationship with that aspect of myself—the person I once was. As I engaged in my healing process, I became aware that I was dealing with my inner child at various stages of my youth—as a baby, a toddler, a young girl, and a teenager. The pain of those hurt, betrayed, and abandoned "children within" was frozen in time, needing to be healed.

Part of healing my inner child has involved re-parenting, giving myself those things that as a child I did not get from my parents. This has meant providing myself, including my inner child, with nurturing, affection, and recognition. To nurture my inner child I had to learn how to play and even to understand that it was all right to play. I had to create a sense of security about my life to reassure that childlike aspect of myself that was so mistrustful. I had to reinforce in myself the fact that I am worthy and that I am lovable. I had to learn not to react to the constant criticism I heard as a child, and to re-parent myself to accept me just the way I am.

For me, the process of healing my inner child was threefold. First, I had to learn to be sensitive to the childlike aspect of myself. This meant learning to "listen" to and believe what my inner child was telling me about those needs that had not been met because of the abuse. Initially, to understand this part of myself, I found it helpful to visualize my inner child at various ages, and to tap into the feelings I had at that time. I recalled and observed many of my early memories, not through my adult eyes, but through the eyes of myself as a child, and I experienced the pain that I had endured as that little girl. I came to understand that I had carried the negative emotions attached to these early events into my adult life, along with the needs that had never been satisfied during my childhood. Today, I still listen to and believe my inner child. For that is what a good parent does.

Next, I let my inner child know that I would do my best to protect myself and also protect her—the same way I so diligently protected my own daughter. Since I had not always taken the best care of myself in the past, the child within me trusted no one—and that included me. At times during the healing process—for example, my first night at the Healing Center—my inner child became extremely frightened. Even today I can feel the childlike part of me get scared when I speak up about my past, and at those times I need to tell myself that I am helping a lot of other children, and that talking about the past does not mean I will be punished for it. I let my inner child know that I have done everything in my power to remain safe. For that is what a good parent does.

And finally, I let my inner child play—not every time that part of me wants to, for at times I do have to work. But I have learned to recognize my inner child's needs. The little girl within me is always there—ready to play, ready to talk, ready to be a kid. I can be remiss at paying enough attention to this important part of myself, but I am working to be better at that. And even when it is not time to play, I always let my inner child know I love her and that I will play later. For that is what a good parent does.

I realize that my inner child is not yet healed, and I understand and accept this reality. Most importantly, I love that aspect of me no less because it is wounded. When desires and impulses arise from the hurt, mistrust, anger, and unworthiness of my childhood, it is not always easy for me to immediately recognize that is what is happening. If I act on impulses that come from these unhealed aspects of myself, I behave childishly, and I am doing myself and my inner child an injustice. Today I still find myself reacting in this manner, in spite of the insight I have gained. The difference is that now I am aware sooner of how I have acted and I can do my best to make amends. Childhood abuse can explain our inappropriate actions, but it does not excuse them. Today I work at meeting the healthy needs of my inner child, and modifying my behavior as it relates to any unhealthy needs. For that is what a good parent does.

I have repaired many parts of my lost childhood. In doing so, I realize how vulnerable I was back then, even though I tried so hard to always be strong. In the process, I have found an innocence that was deeply buried and that I did not know existed. I discovered these things as I re-parented that little girl still inside me. I did it for her—and I did it for me.

❧ OUR EXPERIENCES ❧

I have met other survivors of abuse who pursued their personal road to recovery without the need to recall any of the specific details relating to their abuse. That is not the path I have chosen. By nature, I am an inquisitive person with a need to know. I chose a course of healing that required obtaining the details of certain past events so that I could comprehend more fully the reasons behind the resulting emotional pain I carried into adulthood. That was my process, and I understand that it may not be appropriate or necessary for other survivors.

As much as recalling details is important to me, I have learned that in remembering my experiences the true meaning is found in the emotional truth of an event, not in remembering every miniscule detail of it. I have learned that the emotional truth is how I felt about what happened to me, and that sometimes I have repressed those feelings, and sometimes I have repressed my memory of the entire event. I have found that by allowing myself to remember an event in whatever detail I can, and to feel the feelings I associate with that event, I could begin to accept what had happened. For me, remembering, reliving, accepting, and experiencing the emotions attached to an incident provides the framework in which healing can begin.

I have learned that if we do not have the benefit of a sibling or another credible witness who can acknowledge the abuse at the time it happens, or at a later date, we often rewrite our original experience into a story that is less painful. Sometimes, the society we are brought up in conspires to recast an event, often in simple and ordinary ways. Maybe it was the neighbor who said nothing, the teacher who looked the other way, or the stranger who walked right by us as if nothing were occurring when we were being abused. We start to believe that if no one else saw or heard what happened, it must not have occurred. This new version of the story, based on the reactions of others, replaces the actual story, and we can then carry that revised tale forward for a lifetime. I understand now that however we may have recast a story to make it less painful, the authentic story also remains with us, waiting for us to recall the feelings related to it when we are ready to heal.

Remembering an event is an interesting phenomenon in and of itself. I do not believe that any two people ever experience or remember an event in the same way. I have also come to understand that we do not even remember all of the details of what we have experienced in the same way each and every time we recall or talk about it. People who were in our life at the time of a particular experience may not remember the same details that we do, and they may not recognize the emotional impact that the event had on us. They may not remember the experience at all or they may say that they do not because it is simply too painful for them to acknowledge.

I know now that we all remember what we want to remember, what we need to remember, or what we have the capacity to remember. Another person's not remembering an event does not mean the experience is untrue. By going through my process, I gained trust that the emotions relating to my stories were real, so I did not dwell as much on the literal details, nor did I keep waiting for my brother, sister, and mother to remember them. I found a tremendous sense of freedom in that realization.

If our parents abused us, there is a natural tendency to type-cast them in the roles of villains. If we have not gained an understanding of the circumstances that led them to act as they did, often we decide that they intentionally set out to harm us. I used to think this, and at a certain point I cast my parents as enemies. I no longer believe that characterization is accurate or appropriate. My experience has led me to believe that many parents, mine included, were emotionally damaged children themselves, repeating behavior that they learned from their parents and that occurred in the generations that preceded them. They may have been bad at parenting, but they were not villains. If others abused us, I believe that in many cases they too were abused, and they are repeating what was done to them because they never became aware enough to heal and change their behavior.

Over the years, I have wondered if there were other incidents of abuse in my childhood that I do not remember. While at first I wanted to remember everything and in as much detail as I could, I have come to believe that some of the things that happened to me are too sensitive for me to deal with, and that it may be in my best interest not to recall them. I think I have looked at enough terrifying and shocking circumstances to last me the rest of my life. Still, I believe the remembrance of these painful experiences is a great gift. Sometimes I will purposely recall my memories of being abused as a way to remind myself that if I could survive that, I could survive anything else that life throws at me.

I think the adage that "timing is everything" is true. We begin to work on ourselves when the time is right for our healing, and we will recall memories when the time is right for them to be remembered. All of our early experiences of pain and suffering are stored somewhere, waiting for the right time to be revealed to us, if recalling them is a necessary part of our healing. Some of our memories are deeply repressed or forgotten because they are too terrifying to remember. We seem to have a guardian angel that withholds this information from us until we are able to process it.

For me, the most important realization I have come to is that the abuse I experienced matters. It matters because my responses to that abuse made me who I became as an adult. Until I became aware and understood the ways in which the abuse affected me, I was incapable of making conscious choices to heal the effects of the abuse and to create a better life for myself. I believe that for survivors of abuse, this is a vital part of the healing process. We need to connect the dots between what we experienced in our childhoods and how it led to our beliefs about ourselves and the world and how we act and react. We can then recognize that we have a choice about whether we will continue to act as if we were still abused children, or whether we will re-parent and heal ourselves and act as the whole, powerful, loving adults we can be.

❧ REFRAMING THE PAST ❦

As I continue my process of healing, I have come to understand how I allowed my beliefs about my past experiences to psychologically imprison me for much of my adulthood. For example, I associated North Dakota with hurt, anger, and sadness. To me, family gatherings always meant discord, jealousy, and tension. And while I had experienced these feelings in the past when we had gotten together, the unhealthy disconnect was that I believed the same disaster would occur every time I visited North Dakota or encountered the members of my family. I understand now that it is not the place, person, or activity that is the source of the strong feelings in me. It is the negative beliefs about them that I have held on to.

Once I realized I was doing this, I recognized that I had an opportunity for reframing how I saw the places, people, and situations with which I had strong childhood associations. Reframing means examining situations with a level of detachment, especially those that we have perceived as harmful or even dangerous, so that we can interpret them from a healthier, adult point of view.

I have also needed to reframe experiences that I have associated with the issue of abandonment. Before I became aware of how this issue affected me and sometimes caused me to act inappropriately, I would view any sign of rejection, disapproval, or criticism as a form of abandonment. In countless situations, I could detect one of these signs, even if it was not there. For example, I could decide that a friend who had forgotten a luncheon date with me had disrespected and deserted me. The reality was she had just forgotten the date or the time.

Even after years of working on this demon, at times I still allow it to creep into situations where it is not relevant to the circumstances. When my mind is going full throttle and I cannot adjust my thinking immediately, I make a concerted effort not to run away from a situation that I am reacting to in this way or to make an inappropriate, insensitive, or improper comment. I let the discomfort settle in, knowing I need to address the situation at a later time, when I have had the opportunity to evaluate my response and see if it was appropriate. Sometimes I reach for my copy of *The Four Agreements* by Miguel Ruiz and read (and reread) the chapters "Don't Take Anything Personally" and "Don't Make Assumptions." I love that book, and it is a permanent part of my library. Its words remind me that unpleasant situations are opportunities for me to focus on what still needs healing and opportunities for personal growth.

In therapy, I learned that as an adult, it is exclusively my responsibility to create either my personal freedom or my personal prison. I have discovered that the process of re-framing my thoughts helps me to take back the power I had lost during my dysfunctional childhood. Sometimes I have reframed my views of childhood experiences so that instead of seeing them only in terms of damage and destruction, I see how a situation was a catalyst that led me to develop qualities that I value in myself.

After a lot of practice in reframing, I have gained perspectives that help me to make decisions about where I want to go and who I want to be with, not based on past beliefs, but on a rational assessment of the current reality. I am better at doing this now than I have been in the past, but when it comes to always remembering to use this process, I am a long way away from being great at it! The most honest statement I can make today is that I know I have the capacity to enter into a higher state of consciousness relating to my actions and reactions, even when I do not always do so. When I remember to stay attentive to my thoughts and the related emotions, my life is easier, smoother, and more peaceful.

❧ PARENTING ❧

I applaud anyone who takes on the challenge of being a good parent, and I deeply admire those people who parent well in spite of their history of abuse. The voice of the critical parent that I heard during my childhood, and that kept talking to me throughout much of my adult life, led me to believe that I could never be a good parent. This message turned out to be wrong, as I did manage to function pretty well as a mother. My daughter Angela is now an adult, and I am profoundly grateful that we are very close. I did make mistakes as a parent, and as I have become more aware of how the abuse I experienced in childhood influenced who I became as an adult, I have also become more aware of how it influenced me as a parent. I work at not beating myself up for my mistakes. I understand now that when my daughter was growing up, I was in the midst of my healing process and I did not have the wisdom I have today. I offer the following examples of my lack of awareness at the time, as they are poignant to me.

My in-laws were great at attending many of the after-school events in which Angela was involved, such as dance and athletic activities. I was not always good at showing up. When I was growing up, my parents were not interested in what I was doing and, quite frankly, I remember thinking I did not care if they showed up or not. Having never experienced my parents' supporting me in my activities, it did not occur to me that it might be important for me to actively support my daughter's interests. I was wrong. Subsequently, I discovered that even though she loved her grandma and grandpa, it was me that Angela wanted at the dance recital or watching as she played that game of softball.

Vowing not to repeat the physical abuse I had experienced in childhood, I made the conscious decision that I would never hit my daughter, and I never did. But I did not realize that by not supporting her in her activities, without being aware of what I was doing, I would be repeating the neglect I had experienced.

One summer when Angela was a teenager and home from boarding school, we got into an argument over her "smarting" back at me, as my mother would have called it. I told her, in no uncertain terms, that she was a disrespectful, spoiled brat. She screamed that she could not stand living with me and that she wanted to go live with her father. I screamed back at her, "Well, let's go in and pack your bags." I am still embarrassed and humiliated as I write this, as I understand now that she was engaging me in a battle to find out where her boundaries were. Instead, I unconsciously chose, at least temporarily, to engage in abandoning her, much the same way as my Grandma Blanche and my Aunt Ruby had been abandoned by their parents when they were teenagers. Angela did not go to live with her father. After our heated words, each of us cooled off, and she did not bring up the subject of moving to her father's again. But not being conscious of the potential harm inherent in reacting as I did, I did not apologize. I am grateful that Angela had the maturity that she did, and that we were able to reconcile the situation, even without my having the wisdom to apologize for my angry words and my apparent willingness to send her away just for talking back to me.

When I was growing up, arguments between my father and my mother had two predictable outcomes. My father would leave the house and my mother would not speak to him, often for up to a week or more. As I look back, I find it interesting that when my husband and I argued, I did not follow in my mother's footsteps and use the "silent treatment" on him. I think this was true for a couple of reasons. First, Paul and I argued very little, and, secondly, he would never have tolerated that behavior from me, as he was not raised in family environment in which silence was used as a weapon. However, when Angela and I engaged in a typical teenage mother/daughter struggle during her visits from school, I pulled my mother's old trick out of the hat and would often go into my room and lock the door, refusing to come out to speak to her, even when she knocked on the door and begged me to talk to her. Angela had never observed this behavior in me while her father and I were married and raising her together, so I am sure it was confusing and terrifying to her. The letter she wrote me at fifteen, which I quoted earlier, addresses this very issue. In it she tells me that when I shut her out this way, it only made her angrier, and that she needed me to come out of my room and work things out with her.

Today, instead of feeling guilty about all the mistakes I made, I try to be a better parent to my grown daughter by nurturing and supporting her. I also work hard at becoming an inspiring role model for her. And as I become aware of the mistakes I made as a parent, I acknowledge and discuss them with Angela. I believe all parents make mistakes, and that a healthier, more authentic approach to raising children involves letting them know that we recognize that we are not perfect and that we are trying to be a better person and a better parent. I would rather err on the side of a little painful honesty than rely on trying to present myself with an unrealistic façade of all-knowingness.

Many parents write letters to their children to be read after they have passed away. I opted to write my daughter a letter during my lifetime, which I did several years ago. Angela gave me permission to include that letter in this book.

Dear Angela,

I have said it many times, and I have written about it in this book. No matter what else I do in life, and notwithstanding anything else I achieve, raising you will always be my greatest accomplishment.

My prayer for you, if you decide to have your own children, is that you will take advantage of the positive parental skills I used, and ignore the ways I could have done things better, like being so overprotective.

If I had one piece of advice for you, it would be to shower your children with every ounce of love you have and every minute you can spare. The love you give lasts forever; the toys and games you might give them are easily broken and discarded.

I want to share a story that has stuck with me for years. You were about nine years old and belonged to a Brownie troop. You had just earned the last badge necessary to become a Girl Scout, and you were to be awarded it at the final Brownie meeting of the year. You asked me to take you, and I said I could not go, as I had to work that night. I wasn't paying attention, or I would have seen the disappointment on your face.

Since I "could not" attend the event, another Brownie Mom took you to the ceremony. Looking back today, I cannot remember which client's account I worked on that evening, how much money I made, or how late I got home. But I will never forget the look on your face the next morning when you told me I was the only Mom who wasn't there that night. It is etched in my mind for eternity!

I think children can learn as much from their parents' mistakes as from their successes, and that is why it is important for me to share the story of the Brownies with you.

You will always be the brightest star in my life's sky.

Mom

❧ AWARENESS OPENS THE DOOR TO FREEDOM ❧

I have mentioned that the three major steps of my healing process are awareness, acceptance, and forgiveness. Awareness provides us with the foundation for making changes in our life. Indeed, the first step in making any change is the awareness that a change needs to be made. I carried over many inaccurate beliefs and inappropriate ways of responding from my childhood. I have found that a simple, powerful method for evaluating whether a particular belief or way of acting or reacting needs changing is to ask myself, "Does that serve you?" Today I ask myself that a lot. If the answer is, "No, it does not serve me," I understand that I need to change it and that I am the only person who can correct it.

For example, as I have said, I grew up to be a perfectionist. Constantly meeting disapproval from my mother, I sought to perform my school work and everything else outside of my home with perfection as a way of validating my existence and proving to myself that I had worth—things that I did not get at home. I carried this behavior into adulthood, and it provided me with temporary acknowledgement as others proclaimed how "perfectly" I did things. As I began to observe my behavior from a healthier perspective, I saw clearly how much energy it takes to try to reach that unattainable goal. Ultimately, I also noticed that no one needed me to be constantly perfect, and that most people would actually enjoy me more if I did not try to be so exacting. In other words, trying to be perfect did not serve me. So now I work on letting my imperfections show a lot more and I even offer them up as a point of conversation in the context of my self-healing.

I also realize that being mistrustful does not serve me. As a child, I learned that when I turned over my trust to someone, it was often betrayed, and I wound up being hurt again and again, until I trusted no one. I carried these feelings of mistrust into adulthood and into my relationships, friendships, work situations, and even into my parenting. I was always expecting the worst of people, waiting for "the other shoe to drop." Today, I understand that it is impossible to have the kind of fulfilling relationships I value if I am mistrustful, for I know that I cannot truly connect with others unless I am willing to share, and this implies some level of trust. I work on this a lot, and I am getting better day by day.

The field in which I worked was a left-brained world where you were taught to "think things out" or "use your grey matter." There is no doubt that the mind is a wonderful tool—humankind has used it to get us into outer space, to cure diseases, and to invent computer microchips smaller than the head of a pin.

Although the mind is an incredible gift, I believe authentic awareness resides within our spirit, for that is where we can access real guidance. Whenever I need internal counsel, I remind myself to draw on the knowledge available to me by tapping into this source—whether you call it wisdom, intuition or knowingness. Sometimes I am really good at this, many times I am not. When I am in the middle of a difficult experience, the best technique for me is to ask, "What am I to learn from this?" If I am aware enough to do this while I am in the midst of the situation, the answer will come and I do not get caught up in my perception of the negativity. Even if I lose my perspective during the situation, I try to remember to seek guidance from within after the event has occurred. When I do this, I am able to access the information I need, and in this way I have the opportunity to look at the situation from another perspective, evaluate my actions, and see what I can learn from the experience.

❧ It Had to be Me ❧

I cannot tell you with absolute certainty that I understand all the reasons for the events that occurred in my childhood, yet I did obtain some amazing clarity while on my journey to recover. I believe that one of my missions during this lifetime was to break the cycle of child abuse in my family. An equally important task assigned to me was the telling of my story. My wish is that by sharing my experiences in this book with others, it will bring a sense of hope to those who have gone through or are currently in an abusive situation, and that it will provide assistance to those who are helping children or adults to recover from dysfunctional backgrounds.

It has taken me a long time to come to grips with my childhood and the events that shaped my life. I now realize that all of it was a necessary part of the plan to have me fulfill my purpose in this life. I had to learn about and experience child abuse before I could share my experiences to help others. I am not qualified to write about neuroscience or sailing, for I have no experience with or knowledge about those subjects. On the other hand, I have earned a Doctoral Degree in Mistreatment, an absolutely necessary part of my life so that I could fully embrace my ultimate mission of sharing the story of my journey and my healing.

No longer do I pretend that the things that happened to me did not happen. If I do that, I am denying the very existence of my childhood. In the last few years, I have come to realize that I would not be the person I am today if it were not for my family dynamics. I like who I am today. And since I do, I would be remiss if I did not express my gratitude for the experiences I had and for the courage I was granted to cope with my challenges. I have also come to have compassion for myself and the pain I suffered.

I began to explore my childhood for one reason only—to understand my suffering. I did find out how my childhood experiences affected the suffering I experienced as an adult, yet something even more precious and profound unfolded. When I was able to gain some perspective on the events of my early life, I saw clearly that, although I did not know it at the time, many situations provided an opportunity for my spiritual growth and that each experience offered a lesson. I also learned that it was not the event that had prolonged my suffering, it was the harsh judgments I had placed on myself and others that actually caused the emotional pain to continue. During the time I held these judgments, I actually lengthened the continuation of the abuse, since I remained in a state of anger, resentment, fear, running away, or denial.

I had a lot of work to do to clear a path through my prejudices and assumptions. It has taken me a long time to stop defining an event as good or bad, or right or wrong. That is something I must work on every day. Reflecting on what I learned from a particular event, and how that episode shaped me into the person I am today, has been the most effective method for me to actually change the impact those earlier events have had on my life.

The challenge I faced for a long time was whether I was going to allow the abuse I experienced and the feelings that resulted from it to rob me of the love and trust that were my birthright. Along the way, I realized that only I could determine if that would happen. And finally, I came to the realization that the events of my childhood provided very useful experiences for gaining greater understanding and compassion.

I waited a long time for my father, mother, and brother to explain why they did the things they did. When this did not happen, I waited for apologies that never came. Now I wait for none of that, for I have learned that it is not necessary. I have forgiven all the players in our drama, and I have developed compassion for everyone who was hurt. Most importantly, I have included myself in that process. I forgave myself for abusing myself for years and years with my severe judgments of myself, for the picture I painted of myself as damaged, and for the view of myself as a helpless victim. I have learned to love and nurture myself and to respect the powerful, competent adult I have become.

When I first started my journey of healing, I believed that children come into the world at birth in an entirely pure state, bringing nothing with us but our own new life. There certainly is an element of purity in our being at birth, yet I now understand that we also bring with us our entire familial heritage. I have also come to understand that those elements of our ancestral past that no longer serve us or humanity must be abandoned.

My journey did not result in completely rewriting my life story, but I have been able to put it in a new context and create a different ending—or should I say, a new middle. I came to understand that I would not be the person I am without my childhood experiences, because those experiences brought me to where I am today.

I have a vision that long after we are dead and gone, my family members will meet someplace in another dimension. We will "high five" each other and congratulate ourselves for playing out our drama to the fullest, so that our missions could be completed. We will get some kind of Cosmic Academy Award. I offer this idea not as an abstract concept, but as a possibility for the final ending to my story.

Today, rather than being stuck in resentment, I work on living my life in a state of "replacement." I replace secrecy with openness, judgment with acceptance, and fear with love. Some days are better than other days. Some days I am reasonably successful in my endeavors, and some days I fail miserably. Yet I keep working at it, and that is good enough.

There was only one person who could live my particular life, take my heroic journey, and have my unique outcome. It had to be me.

❧ The End of the Book, the Start of a New Chapter ❧

Today, when I remember to stay in that place of gratitude for all the wonderful blessings I have in my life, the difficult times are easier to go through. My challenge is to remember to do this. Sometimes, my memories of the past have brought me to a place as dark and frightening as the cellar in our old house, but I have learned that these tough times do not last forever. If I start to feel that darkness taking over, I remind myself that I do not need to stay there, and I breathe and let the feelings come and go, along with as many tears as want to flow.

When I get caught up in my stuff, I look at how far I have come from the place where I started to the place where I am today. The pieces of my soul that were left back on that farm in North Dakota have been reclaimed. The breaks in my heart have healed, even though there is some scarring.

I have arrived at a place where I want to turn my pain into passion. For me this means being actively involved in creating a world where children are held in the highest of regard. A world where they are honored and protected. And most of all loved. Our future will be shaped to a large extent based on how we treat our children and how we allow all children to be treated. One of the greatest sources of peace and satisfaction in my life is working with children, helping a child to find his or her way or to regain his or her voice.

As I finish writing this book, the little girl within me is beaming. She has been waiting a lifetime to be heard and to have a voice. Together we sob tears of joy and release, as I write the final sentence.

And so, with boldness and courage, crayon in hand, I finish with this request.

"PLEASE LOVE ALL THE LITTLE CHILDREN AND KEEP THEM SAFE FROM HARM."

Marion Elizabeth Witte

❧ AFTERWARD ❧

This book has been a way of remembering and honoring my past experiences. For many of us who have experienced dysfunctional childhoods, the journey to healing requires embracing our past, recognizing those parts that need to be healed in the present, and knowing that all of this will create a healthier future. Our memories never leave us, but they do not have to keep hurting us. Memories last a lifetime, and they can serve the very valuable purpose of reminding us how far we have come.

For any of you who have had difficult circumstances in your lives, I offer you the hope that adversity can be overcome. It is a challenging process, as it takes intention coupled with hard work to make any real progress. It can be done if you want to do it.

I offer my story as a confirmation of my belief that all events and circumstances in life have purpose. Sometimes we find out what the purpose is immediately. Sometimes we spend a lifetime trying to figure it out. And sometimes, I imagine, we never really do know.

I share the knowledge that all gifts do not come in pretty packages. The important ones are not covered by a return policy. And sometimes, when we are in our darkest place, that place turns out to be the gift itself.

And finally, I humbly offer myself as an example that the human spirit can rise above any obstacles presented to it. I know my life has been divinely guided. And if mine has been, then so has yours.

If you are ready to begin a recovery process, here are some options to consider as you pursue a path to identify and then heal from your past experiences.

- Engage the services of a qualified counselor or therapist. Obtain a referral from a responsible source.

- Acknowledge whether you have an addiction. If you do, enter into a recovery program to treat your addictive behaviors.
- Explore inner-child healing techniques with a counselor or therapist who specializes in this type of work.
- If you feel drawn to remember details of incidents that you sense you have blocked from your memory, consider hypnotic regression therapy with a licensed and qualified hypnotherapist.
- Read self-help books relating to the particular kind of abuse you experienced. Obtain recommendations from counselors or other abuse survivors. Attend personal-growth seminars.
- Enter into a spiritual practice that fits with your belief system, whether it is observing a religion, praying, meditating, walking in nature or tending your garden.
- Find a writing or journaling workshop or playwriting class that allows you the freedom to express your feelings.
- Take classes in art, voice, music, theater. All of these can be wonderful healing modalities.

While you are recovering, and every day for the rest of your life, remember to take care of yourself before you take care of anybody else.

- Commit to being as kind and loving as possible to yourself.
- Enjoy some form of relaxation.
- Take time to get out of your head and into your heart and spirit.
- Be passionate about your life, your journey, and your healing!

I bless each of you as you begin, or continue on, your journey to wellness. And, yes, we can heal ourselves, we can help others to heal, and we can heal this planet.

To all of our little children,

Marion Witte

❧ BOOK CLUB DISCUSSION TOPICS ❧

1. "Little Madhouse on the Prairie" begins by tracing the author's family back several generations. What cultural conditions described in the book may have led to child abuse? How has parenting changed over the last several generations—or has it?

2. Did you feel sympathy for the Witte family's hardships? What is the author's attitude toward her ancestors? Why do you think the author wants readers to know about her grandparents' lives?

3. As a culture we tend to romanticize farm life. What is the author's attitude toward life on her family's farm? Does she describe any positive aspects of being left to roam around the farm unsupervised?

4. The author vividly recounts the moment when she realized that keeping a spotless house was more important to her mother than treating her daughter with love. Do mothers today ever feel pressured to put housekeeping over the needs of their family?

5. Was the author's brother to blame for his mistreatment of his sister? At what point did her brother shift from protector to tormentor? Do all families have a member who seems to get more than their share of abuse?

6. The author describes how television shows of the 1950s gave her a window onto a very different kind of family life than the one she knew. Discuss what she saw and whether or not you think television might play a similar role in the life of abused children today.

7. Why did no teacher, friend or family member step in to halt the abuse of the author? Were they unable to see the signs or was it completely hidden from view? What is our role in society when we see child abuse? Do we have an obligation to step forward?

8. What finally caused the author to confront her mother and say, more or less, enough is enough? Why doesn't this bring about the end of the author's misery?

9. To what does the author attribute her drive for perfection and achievement in college? Did it bring her happiness?

10. Were you surprised by the author's relationship to alcohol? What in her history led her to take a pledge of sobriety?

11. The author's in-laws provided loving parental role models. She tells a touching story of how her own daughter's smudgy fingerprints were left on her mother-in-law's sliding glass doors for weeks as a precious reminder of the little girl. How does the way in which we were parented influence our own parenting? Can we ever completely reject the voices and values that are drilled into us as children? Have you ever heard yourself say something to your children that was exactly what your mother would have said?

12. The author leaves her seemingly wonderful husband to embark on a journey to heal herself. How did you feel about this unorthodox choice? Respect? Censure? Have you ever had to make a similar choice?

13. Of the many paths the author traveled to heal from abuse, which seemed to have worked the best? Why?

14. As the healing process begins to give the author perspective on her life, do her attitudes towards her mother, father and brother change? Discuss the role that forgiveness plays in her struggle to be whole.

15. The author confronts a woman who is abusing her child at a department store. What action do you think the author hopes people will take as the result of reading "Little Madhouse on the Prairie"? What would you do if you saw a child being abused in public?

Breinigsville, PA USA
15 September 2010
245395BV00003B/2/P